Black Man

A Novel
by Amirah Bellamy

Black Man

Black Man. Copyright © 2015 by Amirah Bellamy. All Rights Reserved. Printed in the United States of America. No part of this book may be used or reproduced in any manner whatsoever without written permission except in the case of brief quotations embodied in critical articles or reviews.

For information contact amirahbellamy@gmail.com.

Black Man

Black Man

is dedicated to all the melanated people of the world on their rise and coming into their awakening. May you continue to evolve and hear the call of your spirit.....

Acknowledgments

I thank all of those among the seen and unseen who have helped me to bring about the manifestation of truth, justice and righteousness in my life. Without you I couldn't do any of this. Continue in bliss….

Black Man

Black Man

1

The "N" word. N-G-R (God). Net-tyr. Negus. Negashi. Niger. Negre. Negro. Nigger. "What up my nigga!" "Nigga please!" "No Niggers allowed." "Be a good nigger and do as you're told." "Niggas ain't shit!" "That's that nigga shit." "Nigga you betta back up off me!" "Fuck that nigga!" "I ain't yo nigga bitch!" "Look at that stupid nigger." "Who the fuck you think you callin a nigga!" "Dat's my nigga!" "That bitch ass nigga!" "Sup nigga?" "What's cracka lackin nigga?" "Wuzup niggas?" "You's my nigga!" "My nigga, long time no see." "Faggat ass nigga," "Nigga stop fakin."

2

Nigga sat in the courtroom looking solemnly around the room straight into the eyes of all the faces staring back at him. Some of the eyes staring back were those of the judgemental ones who had already in their minds tried, convicted and sentenced him to death. Others were those of pure hatred who saw him as everything that they deemed wretched in the world. Then there was the one pair of eyes in the entire courtroom that showed him love, pure unadulterated, genuine love for all that he was to her.

The judgemental ones believed that Nigga deserved all that he had coming and to them even that wasn't enough to justly punish him. In their judgemental minds there were certain rules that had to be followed and as far as they were concerned Nigga had broken every last one of them. Therefore, without even knowing him or the details of his case the judgemental ones believed that Nigga should be justly punished. So they watched

Black Man
and waited all the while sealing his fate with their eyes.

The hateful ones saw Nigga as an abomination that needed to be extracted from the earth. They thought to themselves that if the judge didn't adequately punish Nigga they would. The sight of him was sickening. He was the curse of man. He was everything that they hated in the world, a young, black, defiant, hot-headed, uneducated, deadbeat father who didn't deserve to continue to enjoy the privilege of life. To them Nigga was the thing, the germ that infected the world. So they believed wholeheartedly in the justness of their hatred towards him. In their minds, by thinking in such a way all they were doing was bravely stepping up to take what they viewed as a highly toxic germ out by any means necessary.

Meanwhile, the one pair of eyes in the room who loved him saw Nigga as a divinely righteous brothah doing what it took to come into his light. She saw her hero. She saw a God who was rising out of her magical waters finally ready to reclaim his crown. She admired his strength for having overcome so many lifetimes of the adversity that had come at him from so many directions and in so many forms.

Then there was his mother, who was the first of those to utterly despise Nigga seeing him as

Black Man
everything that had ever caused her grief. This was mainly because everything about Nigga reminded her of a long list of men from her past that had in one way or another caused her pain. The list began with her father as well as Nigga's father. In Nigga's mother's mind both her father and Nigga's father were the two men that had ruined her life and as a result she blamed them for everything else that went wrong in her life.

To her Nigga reflected all of their negative qualities including anger, fruitless efforts to establish themselves in the world as men, unfulfilled dreams of making the lives of their children better, unyielding refusal to follow societal rules or give up, unwillingness to compromise on their principles, unrealized personal desires, fearlessness, what she perceived as unhinged opinions, too much focus on influencing the community and not enough on matters of the home and overconfidence.

Then after his mother, educators stepped up to grab the baton in the race to debase NIgga. Doing everything that they could to break his confidence they kept him shut out. Seeing his brilliance they called him a disorder from attention deficit, dyslexia, dysgraphia, language processing disorder to various other mental illness labels. Coming up with a new label every year to keep him bound they did all in their power to keep him from

Black Man

progressing. They put him with the slow learners to convince him that he lacked intelligence. They subjected him to measurements of his intelligence that casted a shadow on his Godliness. Worst of all they taught him that historically he did not exist and was therefore not relevant in society.

Next in line was the black woman. She too had endured much pain and had struggled alongside Nigga. However, somewhere along the way she grew tired of standing beside him as his support and instead took on the role of his adversary.

So the black woman fed into the lie that he did not love her. She started to believe the stories being fed to her that Nigga was nothing but a trifling, lazy, good-for-nothing loser who didn't deserve her respect. She wondered why he couldn't just get himself together and be the man she needed him to be. She didn't understand why he couldn't give her the material lifestyle that she wanted and that her white counterpart had.

The black woman wanted Nigga to make her feel secure and when he didn't do so in a way that was to her liking she struck back and she struck back hard. She pulled out her weapons and launched what was the most viscous of all the attacks that Nigga had endured.

Black Man

She turned his children against him. She made the police her body guard and 911 became her best friend. She joined forces with the judges and got them to send Nigga to his new home in prison. Then she told the media to spread vicious rumors of his incompetence. Yet, her most deadly weapon of all was the hatred that she began to secretly harbor for Nigga that would later destroy us all. It was indeed the black woman's hate for Nigga that would sting the worst.

Then, as if those combatant forces were not vile enough the black woman was followed up by several among his peers who would betray him, steal from him and murder him. They would snitch on him, set him up and do whatever it took to eliminate whom they perceived as the competition.

Then there were the social systems that had waged an all out war against him. This included a long list of adversarial systems such as the government, the marketplace, the health care institutions, the workplace, his culture and even his family.

Yet despite the challenges of facing all of these forces that had so brutally come up against him Nigga knew that each and every one of them had been created for the sole purpose of making him stronger. Nigga just had to maintain his will to hold on long enough until the rest of the black

Black Man
community came into the realization of the truth that he had come to remember.

Having survived the onslaught of battles that he constantly found himself fighting Nigga knew within himself that he was still more than deserving of all the world's glory and all the world's praise. As far as he was concerned the world owed him a gold medal for being who he was and they would soon give it to him whether they knew it or not.

Nigga knew this because *she* had made him remember. So as he looked into her eyes Nigga knew that he was her God Nigga, her All In All, her soul's mate. She gazed adoringly at Nigga and using her eyes she sent him her love from a million light years. She was Nigga's Earth, his queen, his Goddess and hers was a love that was the greatest force in all of existence.

The old, white judge had just asked Nigga if he had any final statements before he issued his ruling. Nigga was in court for yet another child support claim. It seemed that he was a regular there so he already knew the drill.

Nigga had 4 children by 3 different women and they had all come at him playing the child support case card whenever he did not adhere to their bidding. It was the one constant threat that was always held over his head.

So that day Nigga was in court for what seemed like the 40th time and that time he had chosen not to have a lawyer defend him, but had instead represented himself. He had grown tired of wasting his time and money on incompetent attorneys who didn't give a damn about him and only took his case for the easy payday.

When he *did* hire them all the lawyers would do was tell Nigga to accept his fate and pay up assuming that his children's mothers would prevail. Nigga was done putting his fate into the hands of his children's mothers, the lawyers and the judges. He was finally regaining control of his life by representing himself and it felt good.

As Nigga sat pondering his final statements he looked around the room deep in thought about how he had managed to wind up there. It seemed only a memory ago he was a God, at least until it all went horribly wrong.

Nigga sat in quiet reflection of the time when he was a God, a Naga.....

3

Swiftly arising out of the waters they slithered up behind their prey and wrapped their bodies around their necks extracting from them the last of the breath of life. It was what many called the choke hold and how many who came up against them met their fate.

They were the Nagas and they were the most feared warrior Gods in all of existence. They originated from the seventh dimension, which was a parallel earth-like realm. The seventh dimension was very unique because it contained the highest level of human expression as well as the first level of godly expression. It was where the Nagas existed as the python-like Gods who guarded the waters of Nu. They had existed there for several lifetimes.

Meanwhile, down on the third dimension, which was the earthly realm, there lived a savage race. The savage race was bound to the earthly realm and they were bitter about it. They had recently been created for the purpose of awakening the divine ones. So the savage race did everything in their power to make the lives of their 'divine' guest's a living hell. They tortured them, they tormented them and most of all they utterly hated the divine ones.

The divine ones were a race of Gods who lived in the upper realms but who had somehow fallen to what was the most lowly of all existence. In an effort to find a way to cope with the devastation of the fall they had lulled themselves to sleep having erased all memory of who they were. In doing so they also cut off access to most of their Godly powers, which left them defenseless.

Meanwhile, the divine ones tried and tried, though without success, to end their suffering by defeating the savage race. Yet it was all to no avail because they were never able to figure out how to take them down, especially without their powers.

However, there was a couple among the divine ones who had somehow retained much of their memory as well as their powers, particularly their power to communicate to the spirit world. So they remembered who they were and they remembered who the Nagas were. Together they decided that the Nagas were their only hope so they called out to them using their ability to contact beings in other realms. It worked, the Nagas heard their call and had arrived.

It was just after the divine ones had come under heavy attack and were in dire need of assistance. The couple knew that the Nagas were the most well-suited for the job, which was why they called on them. Immediately, heeding their call the Nagas crossed the dimensions to defend.

Whenever there was a need to bring about the death of a dimension in order to rebirth it, the Nagas were called upon. They were also called upon to defend the righteous and destroy the evil. The Nagas also brought civilization to the masses and culture to the world. They had been around since the beginning of existence.

Shortly after crossing over into the third dimension one among the Nagas named El Naga, whom the others looked to as the elder among them, had captured the leader of the savage race. As was one of their war strategies, he had spared the leader's life for the moment.

It was a common war tactic to keep captured leaders alive and well preserved until returning them to their township. Then upon their return, the enemy captive would be slain so as to be made an example of. This was done so that the others knew that the penalty was death for certain crimes committed.

Black Man

In the present case the crime was using trickery to turn the divine ones against themselves. The savage race had convinced many among the divine ones that he was their lord and master and as such they were to do his bidding. In several instances this meant waging wars against several of their own. So eventually the divine ones divided into several groups each harboring disdain for the other. Soon this turned into further divisions of men against women and older generations against younger generations and so on.

Before long the divine ones were so divided that they were in a constant state of war against one another. Meanwhile the savage race sat back and enjoyed the show that they had so cunningly instigated. Then while they had the divine ones fighting amongst themselves the savage race seized the opportunity to expand its controlling hand over them as well as seize their lands. Over time the situation worsened and it seemed that things couldn't possibly get any worse, but they did.

Eventually the divine ones were able to civilize the savage race, but even that resulted in failure because not long after the savage race began to regress and quickly. After only a short time they had gone right back their savage ways. Savagery seemed to be their comfort zone, their safety net, but to the divine ones it was their torture

Black Man

and it was a torture that would plague them for millions of years to come.

By the time the Nagas had arrived the savage race was invading villages, murdering men, torturing women and children, eating the corpses and destroying the land. All efforts to civilize them were all in vain as it seemed the savage race was simply incapable of living in such a way. They were in a sense without values.

Over time the community of divine ones had come to the realization that the savage race was just too loathsome and abhorrent to civilize. They ate their young, lived in their own filth, ate raw, decayed flesh infecting the world with their disease, had no language and no manner of socialization. They were a race that was simply a lost cause. Though the divine ones tried again and again to civilize them it was always without much of any success. This was even more clearly demonstrated when observing the generations that followed as things only got worse.

For that reason the Nagas were called. A couple among the divine ones figured that things were to the point that the Nagas were the only ones capable of civilizing such a reprehensible people and they knew that the Nagas would successfully be able to do so, but in their way.

Black Man

The Nagas way was indeed a unique one. There had already been several attempts made by the divine ones to do so in their more mild mannered way which was ineffective. Each attempt was met only with hostility, resistance, murder and mayhem. However, the outcome would be very different for the Nagas. Their tactics were full proof and highly revered.

So they had arrived. The Nagas, the great warrior Gods, the dragon kings, the serpent warriors, the mystical ones, the wise ones, the protectors of the realms, the ones who brought death and rebirth had arrived. The Nagas had arrived and things were about to take a drastic turn! The Nagas had arrived! Their arrival meant that the clock began to run against the savage race and their days were from then on numbered.

4

Carrying the captured leader within the grip of his body using just enough pressure to cause excruciating pain just shy of death El slithered down the forest pathway surrounded by the rest of the Nagas. Elders among the Nagas were greatly revered and closely protected. It was a matter of respect and honor. Though highly adept warriors, elder Nagas had a wealth of knowledge that was handed down from generation to generation. This knowledge was in many respects the source of the Naga's strength. It was what made them so impenetrable.

Knowledge, however, was not just something that was communicated from one generation to the next through language. It, like everything else in existence, was communicated on the spiritual plane as well. So because the Nagas existed on the seventh dimension they were very much connected to all other spiritual beings of the universe who also had a wealth of knowledge that far surpassed even that of the Naga. Thus, it was their ability to access the universal knowledge that gave them the advantage. It allowed them to channel several powers beyond their own, powers that third dimensional beings would consider superpowers.

As for the powers that were inherently their own the Nagas had the power of foresight. They could travel across several dimensions. They could manipulate energy. They were shape-shifters. They could transform into light at will. They could physically manifest things. They also had the power of telekinesis.

The Nagas, who had these and other powers were a wonder to the savage race. It was nothing they had ever seen and in their ignorance they were threatened by the Nagas' powers. The savage race responded to the Nagas with hostility as they had responded to everyone they had encountered who appeared the least bit civilized. It was their inability to comprehend anything beyond their own primitive ways that was the true source of their intimidation.

So they launched attacks on the Nagas. The Nagas fought back and did so with a force stronger than anything the third dimension had ever seen. From then on it was an all out war, a test of

Black Man

the will to see who would still be standing. It was warrior against warrior.

Ironically, the savage race was a type of warrior clan much like the Nagas. The difference was that the Nagas fought for a righteous cause as well as to protect the divine, the universal good, truth and justice. On the other hand, the actions of the savage race were purely self-serving. Their history had more than proven that.

The story of the savage race's beginnings was an interesting one. They were still in their infancy as they had only been in existence for 6000 years. One among the divine ones, who was called Yac, had created them in an attempt to help the divine ones find their way home. Yac was a scientist and he had what turned out to be a very profound theory.

Yac believed that what had caused the divine ones to descend was a disease, a germ of sorts. So he set out to cure them by creating a race that was made up of the divine ones essence along the the germ that was plaguing them. Yac figured that by doing this and exposing the divine ones to the germ he could cure them of the germ. He figured that from there the divine ones would

Black Man

awaken, come back into their divine rights and powers and from there figure out a way to get back to the upper realms.

Many among the divine ones strongly opposed Yac's radical views and theories and they considered his experiments wicked and unethical. Nevertheless, Yac continued with his research and experiments and eventually he had isolated the diseased energy source and created a race of beings from it with the intention of more closely examining it. He needed to fully understand every aspect of it's nature in order to rid the divine ones of it. So Yac studied the savage race in the distance, taking notes of how they socialized, their means of survival, level of intelligence and treatment of one another.

However, what he saw was disturbing to say the least. The savage race was more loathsome than anything he had ever seen before and he found that they were very resistant to being civilized. More than that it seemed that the savage race was everything the divine ones found undesirable. They were filled with hatred and the more Yac tried to civilize them the more the savage race displayed their hatred toward their maker and the more rebellious they became. Over time the savage race proved to be all the things they were composed of, which included hatred, thievery, deception and anger. In fact, Yac taught them these things.

Before he died Yac wanted to ensure that his experiment worked so he taught the savage race of the divine one's disease. He then taught them how to skillfully use it against the divine ones and they did. They were a recipe for disaster, a disaster that the Nagas would later have to clean up.

After Yac's passing when the divine ones learned of his creation they were outraged and they immediately captured the savage ones and banished them to some caves in the mountains located in the northern hemisphere of the planet. They thought them an abomination and wanted no parts of them.

However, after some time had passed the divine ones began to regret having confined the savage race to the caves and decided to allow them to come out. Though, to the divine one's dismay when the savage race came out they came out blood-thirsty and warring.

The divine ones immediately tried to civilize them at it worked for a short time. However, the savage race was always a warring race so the only thing that civilizing them did was cause them to find more sophisticated ways to bring about war. Then,

Black Man

as they began to better understand the usefulness of being more civilized they became more cunning.

When the divine ones agreed that the savage race was civilized enough to live among them they allowed them to do so. The savage race even played along all the while planning an attack of a different type. Having remembered what Yac taught them they had planned to attack the *minds* of the divine ones using all the methods of trickery and deceit that they had been taught.

It was during some of their initial days of being out of the caves among the divine ones that they had launched the first of their evil attacks. In their naivete and unwillingness to consider what Yac had tried to warn them of the divine ones never even saw the attack coming.

So the next morning they woke up to find that the savage ones had killed and eaten all of their babies. The divine ones were infuriated and they then banished the savage ones back to the caves. Meanwhile, Yac's creation actually turned out to be the cure to their illness. The savage race was the key to their freedom, Yac's theory was correct and the savage race *was* fulfilling their purpose strengthening the divine ones and making them stronger than ever.

After some time had passed, the divine ones once again allowed the savage race to venture out

Black Man
of the caves and roam freely. Though they continued on with their savagery, they seemed a bit more susceptible to domestication than before. Thus, the divine ones were actually able to tolerate them. It was also the only reason why the divine ones didn't just kill them off especially since doing so would have been quite easy given the fact that they greatly outnumbered the savages.

However, one way that the savages were defective was that for some reason it was difficult for them to reproduce. They also had an aversion to the sun as it burned their skin. The divines ones assumed that there was some specific reason that Yac made them that way so they didn't question it.

By the time the Nagas had been called, the savages had been allowed to roam freely for quite some time. The divine ones agreed to allow them to venture out as long as they saw some signs of improvement. It was further agreed that in the event that they weren't any more civilized they would be banished back to the caves indefinitely.

At the time the Nagas were called the divine ones were on the verge of sending the savage race back to the caves. They had already been granted the agreed upon time to roam and yet there was still very little improvement. So because of their noncompliance there had been a near unanimous decision to send them back.

The savage race could sense that their freedom was being threatened and after having spent so much time free they did not want to go back so they began to resist. Since they had grown quite strong after having been out of the caves they were proving themselves to be rather difficult to control. Thus, they successfully managed to totally change the course of events to their bidding. This put the divine ones at a disadvantage. So in the end the divine ones allowed the savage race to remain and continued to civilize them.

Eventually, the savage race was civil enough to build societies of their own, with the help of the divine ones of course. There were still traces of their savagery, but they were at least able to be tolerated. Then over time the savage race was civilized enough to be left alone to live independently.

During that time they created institutions of their own, a government and made laws to be used to govern their people. Yet despite their advancement their savagery ways still prevailed as they continued to display their savage-like social characteristics namely cunningness, cheating and stealing. It seemed that no matter how hard the

Black Man

divine ones tried, the savage race could not be totally civilized. Soon they got to be so good at their cunningness that they began to infect the divine ones with their savagery.

They were stealthy and clever with their persuasive abilities and had proven themselves quite adept at mind control. In fact, by the time the Nagas had arrived the savage race had managed to convince the divine ones that *they* were the Gods.

Upon seeing this the Nagas clearly understood why the savage race had been created and what had to be done on their part. The divine ones were worse off than they had originally thought. What they were going through with the savage race was necessary. So the Nagas knew that what was to come was the only way that the divine ones were going to snap out of whatever dream state they were apparently in.

5

No one knew of the Nagas presence on the third dimension, not even the divine ones who had called upon them. The Nagas had the ability to be in several dimensions at once, which was what made them so good at what they did. They were everywhere and nowhere at the same time. They could peek into one dimension while remaining in their own. So since the divine ones had not yet seen the Nagas they had no idea that they had arrived.

The Nagas didn't want to alert anyone of their arrival. They preferred to handle things in the shadows. Besides that, they believed it was best under the circumstances. They knew that the divine ones were on a downward spiral and that spiritually they were free-falling. Thus, the Nagas did not feel they could deal with knowledge of such things as beings visiting from other dimensions. So they agreed to maintain invisibility.

Black Man

As was their nature, the Nagas were the ultimate predator focused only on the kill. As a pack they slithered along through the forest cloaked in their mystique seen only by those of the unseen worlds.

The Nagas were a very ancient group of serpent warrior Gods. They were most known for their brute strength, intelligence and fearlessness. None could defeat them and thus they were rarely challenged. Their primary war tactic was one of stealth. They could spring up when one least expected them to and when they did they always had the advantage. This time was no different.

The divine ones who had contacted the Nagas told them that the third dimensional realm was at risk of being taken over by the savage race. They also told the Nagas that in their attempt to rid themselves of an energy that was causing them to descend they created an alternate race derived from their own essence.

Like the Nagas, the divine ones were also ancient Gods. They were from the higher dimensions, higher than even the Nagas. They'd created the earthly realm as a place to purge themselves of an undesired energy that was plaguing them and causing them to descend.

Black Man

The Nagas had made their way to an ancient city called Alkebulan, which was a rich, lush metropolis in the middle of a desert. In Alkebulan resided some of the planet's most ancient beings. Many among them were the original ones who had created then inhabited the planet to rid themselves of the diseased energy that was plaguing them.

Upon the Nagas arrival they briefly looked around observing and making notes of what they saw as obvious things causing the divine ones to descend. What they first noticed was that the divine ones had become servants of their emotions, which was unheard of among beings in higher dimensions. This was causing them to become arrogant and at odds with one another. The savage race saw this as an opportunity to seize control and they did.

Upon observing this the Nagas knew that the purging process had already begun. It began when the savage race was created. Though the divine ones were regressing, ultimately the same would result in their rise. So in seeing this the Nagas knew that the best thing for them to do was to return to the seventh dimension and watch things unfold from there.

The Nagas could foresee that the savage race would bring so much suffering to the divine

Black Man

ones that it would force them into the jolt needed to spring themselves back into their original Godly nature. So the Nagas returned and observed from the seventh dimension. They agreed to give the savage race 6000 years to rule then after that time they would be exterminated and so it was.

6

After the Nagas left it seemed that instantly things took a turn for the absolute worst for the divine ones. Having more in common with the savage race than they thought, the divine ones began to act more and more like them. The divine ones began to lie, cheat and steal. They became disloyal to one another. They began to dishonor one another. They began to disrespect the sanctity of their unions. They began to completely lose sight of who they were in every way possible. Ultimately, they began to transform into the savage race becoming less and less civilized.

The first signs of this transformation was in their new king, Wasir. Wasir, whom all the divine ones highly revered, had allowed all of the adoration that he was receiving from the people fill him with conceit. He began acting as if everyone else was beneath him.

Black Man

Prior to Wasir, Sutekh ruled Alkebulan. However, once the cycle of unrest had returned to the heavens his attention was needed there and so he left Wasir to rule the underworld, known as earth in his absence.

Sutekh was the strongest of all the divine ones and had therefore been assigned by his grandfather, Re, to be guardian of the upper realms. Re knew that Sutekh was the only one strong enough to do it, which was why he gave him such an assignment.

Every aspect of Sutekh's nature exuded strength. He was not only physically strong, but mentally he was strong enough to hold all the knowledge of the universe. On the other hand, Sutekh was also known for his kindness and loyalty. For as strong as he was Sutekh was very loving, which was what the people loved most about him during his rule.

During Sutekh's rule the divine ones stationed on earth flourished. They loved Sutekh and he loved them. It was the spirit of love that helped them to ascend. The love shown to the people by Sutekh was returned to him tenfold and out of love they honored him and did all that he asked of them to build up the planet.

However, things changed when his brother Wasir came to rule. Wasir, unlike his brother, did

Black Man
not rule with love. His manner of ruling was childish. Contrary to his brother, he ruled by keeping the people in a perpetual state of fear of him. So they loved him, but out of fear. He told them that if they loved any other God or placed any other God before him he would be jealous and as a result he would bring his wrath upon them. So the people obeyed.

Consequently, Wasir had become quite the superstar and was loving it. People from lands far and near highly regarded him as their lord and savior. For them he represented all that was truth. He represented what the divine ones came to *think* they needed, which was salvation. This adoration of Wasir had caused the divine ones to descend even further and fast. As the Nagas had observed they were in a spiritual free fall.

The divine ones began to forget the influence of their own power. Instead they began to give all of their power to Wasir and he soaked it up like a sponge. Wasir had become sick with the power that he had amassed from the divine ones and he became drunk with pride.

One day, as he was waking up one morning in his castle in Alkebulan Wasir looked up to find his

Black Man

brother Sutekh staring at him. Sutekh had stopped in to check on Wasir.

Sutekh had been watching Wasir for some time. While he observed him he couldn't help but notice that something was very different about his brother and so he inquired as to what it may be.

"Brother there is something very different about you. Is there anything going on that I should know about? What has happened since my last visit here? And I sense that the others have changed as well. What's going on?" Sutekh inquired.

"Things couldn't be better here brother. What are you seeing?" Wasir replied.

"I'm not sure, but I sense that the energy here is low. It seems you all have undergone descent. You were to continue leading them back to the upper realms, but instead you have driven them down along with yourself," Sutekh said beginning to get irritated.

"What are you saying brother? Things couldn't be better. Look around. I've turned this desert into a lush land. Look at the city. It's heaven on earth and the people are happier than they've ever been. Because of me they have all that they will ever need, want or desire. I am their All and with me they *will* rise. I *have* saved them from their descent," Wasir answered smugly.

Black Man

Looking at Wasir in both shock and disgust Sutekh couldn't believe his ears. "Brother what has gotten into you? You were sent here with a task to get the people back on track, but instead you have lost your way and taken them on a downward spiral with you. You have damned the Gods and for what? All to feed your lowly pride!" Sutekh shouted with a thunderous rumble making the entire planet shake.

"Who are you to speak to me of pride. You who are too good to be down here with the rest of us. When was the last time you visited brother," Wasir snapped back.

"No brother I have not been down here as that is not what I have been commissioned to do. You are supposed to be handling things down here, so it was assumed that I was no longer needed here. Yet, all you've managed to do is make a mess of things. What are you doing brother?" Sutekh rumbled again.

"I'm doing what you with all your so-called brute strength *couldn't* do *brother*. You may be the stronger one, but clearly I'm the smarter. I'm leading these people. You're just mad because I'm doing what you could *never* do. This place has never looked this good. And to think, all this time you had these people so in adoration of you. What a joke!" Wasir sneared.

Black Man

"No brother it is you who are the joke. You really need to pull yourself together or else I will have to intervene," Sutekh ordered and with that he was gone.

When Sutekh returned to the upper realms he was met by his wife, Ese. Ese was known throughout the universe as the great mother-heaven. Along with her husband, Ese ruled the upper realms.

As the counterpart to him she was the most powerful of the Goddesses and was called the mistress of magicians. She earned that title because with her magical powers she did what no other God could. She got Re to tell her the secrets of the universe. It was unthinkable that anyone could ever succeed at doing such a thing, but Ese did.

Though even with all of her magical powers not even Ese had a clue as to what was troubling Sutekh. She felt his rumbling rage long before he even made his way back from the lower realms.

"What is it dear? What's troubling you?" Ese asked Sutekh endearingly as he faded back into the heavens.

Black Man

"I was just down on the earthly realm checking in on Wasir only to find that he has really made a mess of things," Sutekh said in visible frustration.

"What do you mean?" Ese asked not seeming all that surprised.

"Well when I ruled it was just without all the excess egotism. He's down there prancing around like he's the big man in town or something. He's lost focus! It seems he may have even forgotten what he's even supposed to be doing and as a result he's free-falling and taking the others along with him. They're following his lead even though they know better. I just don't get it," Sutekh fumed.

"Oh dear. Are things really that bad?" Ese asked suspecting that Sutekh was overreacting as usual and perhaps even exaggerating things a bit.

"Yes! It really *is* that bad! How dare you question me about that! There you go again! Always with your disbelief and distrust in anything that I say!" Sutekh snapped at his wife angrily.

Sutekh had quite the explosive temper and at times it took the total sum of Ese's nurturing abilities to keep him calm. She usually had patience to deal with it, but more recently she had grown tired of it. Ese looked over at Sutekh angrily. She was becoming more and more disenchanted with him.

Black Man

As she watched Sutekh fume she remembered the time when they were once so in love. It was a memory that seemed so long ago.

Then as she gazed over at him she couldn't help but feel anything but disgust for him. So much had changed between them and even with all of her knowledge she had no idea why. So she responded to him in silence then left him with his thoughts.

Sutekh sat and pondered what he had just seen on Earth and the more he thought about it the more upset he became. He had worked so hard leading the people back toward the upper realms only to have Wasir so quickly ruin it, all just to feed his larger than life ego. Sutekh was growing tired of having to clean up Wasir's messes and he knew that in the end he would eventually wind up having to do the same thing again. He also knew that things were about to get a lot worse, which they did.

7

The next day while Sutekh was up in the heavens still pondering how best to deal with what was going on in the lower realms he wondered what Wasir was doing. It was as if he had purposefully gone and undid everything that Sutekh had done. Sutekh also noticed that Wasir had taken down all structures of Sutekh and replaced them with monuments of himself. It was a spirit of arrogance that was just not typical of Gods in the higher realms. It seemed Wasir had been stricken with a bad case of vanity all of a sudden.

Then Sutekh turned his attention to Ese. He watched Ese suspiciously sensing that something too had changed about her. It seemed that all around him things were changing. It was clear to him that the universe was shifting and so he decided to focus on how best to address the apparent shift.

Meanwhile, Ese sat deep in thought about things she preferred to keep secret from Sutekh.

Black Man

Ese had always been a woman of many secrets. After all she, accompanied only by Re, held knowledge of all the universal secrets.

"What has you so enraptured in thoughts over there my queen?" Sutekh queried.

"Oh nothing of the matter my king," she answered blankly.

Sutekh wondered if he had gone too far the day before. He knew that many times in his rage he could alienate Ese, but he also knew that she was usually able to calm him in a way that most others could not. For that he loved her immensely. He just wished that she knew that. He often also wished that she too showed him the same level of love, loyalty and dedication. To Sutekh she always seemed miles away so he could never quite figure how she truly felt about him. What he did know without a doubt was that Ese had secrets. He also knew that soon enough some of those secrets would be revealed.

"So what do you say to us doing something romantically fun today? I was thinking a trip to star Bliss might be fun," Sutekh suggested figuring that perhaps a trip might put them in a better space.

"Hmmm I don't think so. I already planned to tend to some things in the underworld today," Ese replied nonchalantly.

Black Man

"Oh really. I thought you had tended to all of your duties in the underworld. What more do you have to do there?" Sutekh asked curiously.

"I still have to nurture the planet dear. It's still in its infancy you know," Ese answered.

"Well based on what I saw yesterday I don't think your nurturing is any longer needed. What I saw there does not need nurturing so you will not make any additional trips there for now is that clear?" Sutekh ordered.

"You are not the nurturer my king so what do you know of what does and doesn't need my nurturing. Besides that, there is no life in existence that doesn't need that from me," Ese said defensively.

"Well you can save that for me. As you know I am always in great need of your nurturing. It's what keeps me balanced my love," Sutekh said coyly.

"Oh is that so," Ese responded seemingly a bit annoyed.

Ese knew what Sutekh was eluding to. He was feeling a romantic way. However, she was simply not in the mood. At the same time, she knew that he would keep pushing until she allowed him to have his way with her so she decided that rather than enrage him by declining his requests she'd do better to appease.

Black Man

Later that day they went on a trip to star Bliss. Ese made it clear that she wasn't particularly excited about things, but Sutekh nonetheless tried his best to make the trip fun. Though no matter what he tried he noticed that Ese still seemed to be miles away. The longer they stayed the more Sutekh felt estranged from her. He was beginning to run out of ways to get Ese close to him. Sutekh was beginning to wonder if things would ever return to what they once were with his wife.

For some time it seemed that when they made love it felt loveless. When he did things to show her love she seemed unmoved. When he stood lovingly at her side she turned away from him. It seemed the very existence of him was an annoyance to her and he could not figure out why.

Nonetheless, Sutekh and Ese enjoyed the remainder of their trip as best they could before heading back to the upper realms. Then, just moments after they returned Ese, like the mistress of magic she was, mysteriously disappeared.

8

Back on earth Wasir was enjoying his kingdom to the fullest. He had never known such pleasure. He was soaking up the energy from everyone's love faster than they could produce it and he was transforming it into power. Power began to fill his veins and an unquenchable thirst for it began to consume him.

His wife, Nebet, though concerned about the change in him still stood by his side ruling along with him all the while exemplifying a flawless image of the loyal, dutiful wife. Nebet, unlike her sister, Ese, adored her husband. She loved him often to the point of blindness. In many ways Nebet and Ese were polar opposites of one another.

"Is there anything that I can do for you my king?" Nebet asked before preparing to venture into the community to comfort some among the divine ones whose loved one had recently transitioned to the even lower realms.

Black Man

"No dear. You're too good to me. With you I want for nothing," Wasir answered endearingly.

Meanwhile, unbeknownst to Nebet, but known to Wasir Ese was waiting to speak to Wasir. For some reason she felt it necessary to cloak herself from her sister's sight so Wasir figured it best to play along. He quickly devised a plot to get Nebet to be on her way.

"Hmmm it might be nice to have a prepared evening of entertainment later if you can manage to pull that all together my queen," Wasir said coyly.

"Of course. Anything for you my magnificent king," Nebet gleamed and with that she was off.

After Nebet had left Wasir was anxious to find out what was the matter with Ese. He also wanted to know why she was hiding from her sister. Usually they were quite close and he hadn't heard anything of them having a spat so he was anxious to learn why Ese was being so secretive. Though secretive and Ese tended to go together as everyone well knew.

Looking about the room waiting for Ese to get rid of her magical cloak of invisibility Wasir called out, "You can come out now my lady."

"Hmmph as if you know me so well," Ese said with a smirk as she slowly began to fade into view.

Black Man

"I do indeed. So what brings you down here with the lowly dear queen of the heavens?" Wasir said sarcastically.

"Well I heard that you were troubled and came down to see if I could lend my services," Ese answered.

"Oh is that so. I gather it was your husband who informed you of this? I suppose ones' being 'troubled' is in the eye of the beholder. As I told your husband, I couldn't be better. Have you looked around? The lands are more fertile than they've ever been. The divine ones are happy and prosperous and I have never before experienced such pleasures. So what is there of trouble here?" Wasir responded.

"My, I guess if you put it that way looks like things are just grand down here. Looks like you've created a mini heaven on earth from what I can see. So tell me, how did you do it?" Ese inquired.

"Always the inquisitive one you are Ese. I won't reveal to you my secret, at least not willingly. Though we both know you have your ways of getting information that you want," Wasir answered half jokingly.

"I do indeed. I do indeed," Ese said and with that she was gone.

Wasir knew that wouldn't be the last that he would see of Ese. He sensed that something was going on with her. Perhaps there was something troubling her or she just wanted some time away from the heavens. He couldn't call it, but he knew that she would be back.

After Ese left, Wasir decided to go out into the courtyard of the castle. He needed some air. Besides that he needed a dose of some of the love of the divine ones. It became like a drug to Wasir and he began to crave it insatiably. Wasir had become vampire-like. He was changing for the worst and it was happening quickly.

As expected, the instant Wasir entered the courtyard he was surrounded by people eager to show how committed they were to him and prove their love. Wasir was particularly fond of the adoration of the women among them and invited a few to join him in the castle. There he would allow them to explore their imaginations as they waged competitions against one another to see who could demonstrate their love for him the most creatively. Meanwhile, what Wasir did not know was that one of the women was in disguise.

Once Wasir had made his decision as to who he wanted to join him they all made their way into the castle. He has selected three who were among the most beautiful. Wasir believed that beautiful women were dishes best served to him and it was a dish that he partook in often. In that way he and his brother were polar opposites as Sutekh only had eyes for his wife, Ese.

The castle had many wings and Wasir had a private wing built where he went to do what he considered, enjoying the pleasures of his kingdom. Wasir's private wing was even more heavenly than this master wing. Guests who were so honored as to visit it were amazed by the grandeur of the wing.

It was underground yet it looked like a beautiful garden. It was the most breathtakingly beautiful garden that any had ever seen. There were lush trees, grass and the most beautiful fragrant flowers that came in all colors. There were fruit trees that had the sweetest, exotic most mouthwatering fruits that anyone had ever before eaten. It was in all respects the most beautiful place in the world.

Wasir created it after his powers had grown. He had been experimenting with them a bit and eventually used them to create his private wing. The wing was created using the power of illusion, which he'd learned from his wife. Ese may have been known as the mistress of magic, but Nebet was magic's queen-mother.

In her love and adoration of her husband, upon his request she would share with him much of her knowledge of such crafts. In turn, Wasir was using this knowledge to create a world of his own

Black Man

starting with his private wing, which not even Nebet knew about.

As Wasir looked around admiring his creation even more so than his beautiful guests, one among them caught his attention. Instantly, he stopped to look at the woman standing nearest to him and asked, "And what do you call yourself?"

"I am Aya," she answered seductively.

"Hmmm impressive," Wasir replied before turning to the next to the right of Aya.

"And what about you dear one? What is your name?" Wasir asked the second woman who was even more stunning than Aya or any other woman he'd ever laid eyes on.

"I am Nubi," she answered. The moment she spoke, Wasir was absolutely mesmerized by her. In fact, he could not take his eyes off her.

"You two be gone. I have what I want now," Wasir said to the other two women without breaking his gaze from Nubi.

Hurriedly, the other two women heeded his command and left the castle.

"So Nubi let me first say that you are....."

"stunning," Nubi said completing Wasir's sentence while looking at him intensely.

"Yes! And I see you read minds too? Is that one of your gifts?" Wasir inquired.

Black Man

"Yes it is one of many, my king," Nubi said gazing at Wasir seductively. "In fact, I can show you some of my others.... if you like," Nubi suggested.

"I would love that indeed," Wasir said grabbing Nubi by the hands as he stepped backwards to lie on a nearby pillow.

"Your wish is my command," Nubi said slyly.

As Wasir plopped down Nubi turned around so that her back was toward him. She then used her power to create some music and while the music played she slid and wound her body like a snake.

After only a few seconds Wasir could not contain himself. He instantly began to desperately crave the woman. He'd never wanted for a woman so badly before in his life. However, she was intoxicating to him and he could focus on nothing other than possessing her.

In sheer desperation he shouted out to her, "I'd love to see that a little closer my lady. Did you come here only to tease me or to please me?"

"Oh I came here for a little of both," she answered before pausing, then continuing she said, "In time, my king. We are in no rush." Then Nubi continued to wind her body even more seductively than before.

Black Man

    This continued on for another 5 minutes or so as she sauntered over closer to him. Eventually she turned around to face him. When Wasir looked into her eyes he was smitten with Nubi's beauty. The more she wound her body the more he so desperately craved her. As he looked even deeper into her eyes he wanted nothing more that to prove that to her.

    For the moment he forgot about his wife, he forgot about his kingdom and he forgot about his responsibilities. He had created his private wing as an escape from it all and with Nubi there he was more than eager to do just that.

    She was getting Wasir right where she wanted him and she knew it. As Nubi was actually Ese in disguise she thought to herself that Wasir was still so predictable. It was there very thing about him that she believed she needed at the time.

    She had grown tired of Sutekh being such a hot-head all the time always worrying so much about the woes of the world. To Ese, Wasir's ignorance was bliss and a welcomed breath of fresh air. So she decided to have a little fun, something that she hadn't experienced in a long time. With Sutekh it was all work and no play and with that she had grown bored.

Black Man

"Oh why must you punish me this way," Wasir cried out nearly about to explode in anticipation of possessing the Goddess.

"Oh I assure you that this will be no punishment. I just want you to relax my king. Let me serve you. I promise you it will all happen in divine time," Ese said reaching over to whisper in Wasir's ear. Then with that she was gone.

9

Wasir was devastated by Nubi's disappearance. He had commissioned a team of people to find her. She became his obsession. He had to have her. At the same time he was outraged at how she had toyed with him. He decided that once she was found she would be punished for treating him that way at least after he had his way with her.

Day in and day out Wasir thought of nothing else, but Nubi. Noticing the change in him Nebet gently pryed to see what was the matter, but it was to no avail. Wasir's mouth was sealed in secrecy. Nebet decided not to press the issue and figured Wasir would share with her what was wrong in his own time.

Meanwhile, in the heavens things weren't any better between Sutekh and Ese. In fact, things had gotten worse. As Ese began obsessing over Wasir she became even more distant from Sutekh. He tried everything to again captivate her interest, but nothing worked. He tried talking to her more, taking more interest in her activities, expressing his love for her more, spending more time with her, offering to discuss the things she wanted to discuss and he even tried switching things up a bit in their lovemaking to make things more intriguing. Yet, the harder he tried the more distant Ese became. Eventually she turned cold. This made Sutekh angry and his rage grew explosive to depths that not even Ese could subdue.

"What is wrong!" Sutekh grumbled one day as the two of them sat staring into space as if the other was not there. This had become a regular occurrence as the two of them were communicating less and less.

"Nothing my king, why do you ask?" Ese answered calmly.

"Why do I ask?!!??? Are you serious right now?" Sutekh roared making all of the heavens tremble.

Sutekh possessed such great strength that the mere utterance of his voice shook the balance between time and space. So when he yelled it was like a volcanic eruption. Many thought Sutekh scary and unpredictable at times. Things were no different for Ese and she looked at Sutekh having a slight tremble of her own. He'd never gotten so enraged with her and at the moment she had no idea how to restore his calm.

Black Man

"I meant you no disrespect my king. I don't know what's wrong, but surely whatever it is we can cure it together. Perhaps it's the shift We've both felt it. It may be affecting us," Ese suggested in an attempt to calm his mood and restore his faith in her.

"Yeah perhaps," Sutekh responded suspiciously.

Sutekh knew that Ese was hiding something. It seemed that during that time she was just full of secrets. Though as the light bringer he was confident that whatever it was he would soon shed light on it. In the meantime, he decided to give her a pass, but he made it a point to keep a close eye on her. As secretive as Ese was it would take the eye of Re to reveal whatever it was she was hiding.

"So what are our plans for the evening?" Sutekh asked after having managed to again regain his composure.

"Oh perhaps an evening on the Sirius canal would be nice. We could certainly use the healing energies of it right about now I think. It might do us some good," Ese answered.

"Yes, that would be nice. Let's do that," Sutekh answered blankly.

He was not convinced by Ese's sudden change of mood and knew that she was only doing it to placate him. He figured he'd just continue to play along until he revealed her secret.

So that evening they went to the Sirius canal and enjoyed the most romantic of times. Using her powers of seduction Ese managed to restore some likeness of harmony between them. For a while after they even seemed to be back to their old selves flirting with each other more often and consistently having more enjoyable lovemaking sessions.

However, Ese still longed for something more. Something was changing in her and it seemed that Sutekh was just not what she wanted anymore. Though she didn't clearly know what she wanted she knew that it wasn't Sutekh.

Her mind would often wander back to the fun that she had with Wasir that time she disguised herself as Nubi. She wanted so badly to return to earth to complete what she had started. She was enchanted by Wasir and it was a feeling that she wanted to explore further. Unlike Sutekh who was always so serious and mostly concerned about securing the upper realm, spiritual battles and other cosmic affairs, Wasir was a lot more relaxed, adventurous and carefree. He was like a breath of fresh air and she wanted nothing more than to breathe more of him in as her life force energy.

Black Man

10

Back on earth as much time had passed since last he saw Nubi Wasir began to think of her less. After years of looking his team had no luck locating her so he called off the search. It was as if she had disappeared just as quickly as she had appeared. He resolved to try to forget about her though it didn't work. The more he tried not to think about her the more he thought about her.

Wasir had since invited many others into his private wing, but none of them compared to the intriguing mystique of Nubi. He didn't know if it was her mystique or her beauty that captivated him so. He just knew that he had to have her. He figured that perhaps one day she would again return to him.

In the meantime, he continued to develop the planet and teach the people of *his* truths. As the Nagas had foreseen the savage ones had managed to manipulate Wasir and the others into believing that Wasir was their greatest leader ever. The savage ones had basically used Wasir as bait

Black Man

to sedate the minds of the divine ones so that they could later control them enough to eventually do *their* bidding. It was the beginning of what would turn out to be the most seductive, masterful world domination feat ever before witnessed in all of the cosmos.

Before, it was the loving Sutekh that was so highly revered. Then something changed and beliefs began to transform. It was so subtle a shift that went so far beyond anyone's detection that no one even noticed. Former truths began to fade and the divine ones began favoring one God over another, which was totally out of character for them as it was not their way to do such things. As Gods they were all equal and uniquely created to serve a specific purpose. So there was no God that was better than another.

Only the Nagas could see that it was the savage one's doing and as far as they were concerned it was just a lesson that the divine ones would have to learn, all be it the hard way. So the savage race began to position themselves to rule by bringing about social unrest, division and chaos among the divine ones. They were calculated and clever in their movements and stealthily managed to eventually transform the entire belief system of the divine ones replacing their truths with contradictions

Black Man

and lies. It was mind control at it's best and they were the masters of this artform.

Next, the savage race began boosting the ego of Wasir showering him with the illusion of love and telling him that he was a much better ruler than his brother Sutekh had ever been. Wasir fell for it hook, line and sinker.

Despite Wasir's status as a God he in many ways had much in common with the savage race, which was likely the reason why it was so easy for them to manipulate him. Like the savage race, Wasir was bound to the underworld. Also like them he had an insatiable desire to be shown love, fear and adoration. It was the thing that made him feel empowered. Another characteristic that he shared with the savage race was his egotism and strong inclination to being dominated by his emotions. The other Gods were beyond all of that, but because of his indivisibility from the lower realms Wasir in many ways succumbed to and took on the characteristics of that space which made him a prime target for the savage race.

Meanwhile, contrary to his brother, Sutekh wasn't so ego-driven. Though many genuinely loved him he didn't thrive on receiving their love. Nor did he ascend as a result of it. The source of Sutekh's power was his own internal knowing. Sutekh had not been enslaved by his emotions or the humanness of being on the lower realm of earth. Unlike Wasir, earth's gravitational pull had no effect on Sutekh and so he was able to maintain a harmonious balance of existence both on earth and in the heavens. Sutekh and Wasir were polar opposites and the savage race had used those attributes to form a wedge between the brothers as well as the divine ones.

In observing from afar what the Nagas had predicted was that the wedge would continue to grow between the brothers ultimately resulting in a catastrophic battle that would devastate the existence of all the divine ones in such epic proportions that it would take them many thousands of years to recover. For that reason, the Nagas knew that their interference was premature so they decided to wait for things to unfold. Only in divine time would they resurface to protect the earthly realm.

Until that time, the savage race would be granted the freedom to use all of their manners of trickery, manipulation and control to invoke the most devastating, traumatic domination ever before experienced in all of the universe. The Nagas were assured that in overcoming this experience the divine ones would eventually be resurrected and come back stronger than ever. It was what the universe needed and it was the reason for the

Black Man
current shift that was being felt throughout all of existence.

So the Nagas patiently watched and waited. Meanwhile, the savage race stealthily made their move and the divine ones along with Sutekh, Ese, Wasir and Nebet all played their parts in the saga of endless suffering that was to unfold.

11

One day, while Wasir was resting the strangest thing happened. To his surprise Nubi appeared to him. It seemed that out of nowhere she just appeared. The door to his room was heavily guarded so he knew that there was no way she got into his room through the door. Nebet had magically secured the room otherwise making it near impossible to enter the room by any means of magic. So Wasir was very curious as to how she got in.

However, just as quickly as his curiosity was peaked it just as soon disappeared as he was again captivated by Nubi's intoxicating beauty. He rolled over from his back and gazed into her eyes as if he was hypnotized by her. Though in a sense he was because Ese was using her powers of seduction over him. She was skillful at such things and there were not many that could resist her.

Then within an instant Ese had transported them to the private wing. The two of them lay upon

Black Man

the same pillow that Wasir laid upon the last time Ese was there disguised as Nubi. This time Nubi revealed to Wasir a little more of her magical powers. She transformed Wasir's private room into an enchanted forest.

All around them appeared the most beautiful lotuses. They were like no other lotuses before seen and in other ways they were quite special. Ese's lotuses gave off the most powerful pheromones, which made Wasir desire Ese even more! He had never wanted anyone or anything that bad in all of his existence. Soon they were literally floating clouds, which Ese had also created then transported them to. As they glided along Ese made manifest several moons that glowed reflecting a hypnotizing light that entranced Wasir lining him up for the kill.

In no time Wasir was putty in Ese's hand. Looking into his eyes Ese knew that she had Wasir right where she wanted him and so she went on and made her move. She proceeded to do just as she had for so long dreamt of doing. Ese loved Wasir without words, without inhibitions and without the fear of consequences.

She forgot about who she was, who he was and what obligations they both had to their spouses. Ese believed that she deserved to be loved in the way that Wasir was capable of loving her. She felt that it was just what she had been missing during all of her time with Sutekh and all of his rage. She needed to feel the kind of love that she believed she just wasn't getting from Sutekh. It was a love that she had so many times observed Wasir giving to her sister Nebet and that she had always longed for. So Ese believed that what she was getting from Wasir was her just due.

With the supreme mastery of her body she invoked in Wasir sensations that she had never even given Sutekh. As she loved Wasir she too became captivated by him. He was quite the masterful lover unlike anything she had ever before experienced. Then as their roles reversed and it was the enchantress who had become the enchanted before Wasir's eyes Ese's disguise faded and he saw her in her true form.

First having a momentary feeling of anger his mood quickly changed to redress. However, the moment he thought about how Sutekh had treated him earlier his anger quickly transformed to fulfillment. Wasir began to feel a sense of vindication for all that he hated about his brother. In his mind Sutekh deserved what he was getting, always putting him down. To Wasir it was good that Ese desired him so. He always wanted her anyway and never quite understood why she had chosen Sutekh over him to begin with.

Black Man

So with thoughts full of vengeance Wasir made love to Ese taking her to greater heights than he had ever before taken any woman including his wife, Nebet. Ese was intoxicated by his essence. She had never known such a love existed and vowed to get her fill of it again and again and again, which she did.

That day Ese and Wasir made sweet, passionate love until they both melted into one another and time and space disappeared. Days had gone by before they finally stopped and when they did separating was as painful as open heart surgery without the benefit of anesthesia.

During that brief time Ese and Wasir had fallen deeply in love with one another. When they were apart they could think of nothing else. So they continued to sneak around for centuries each falling hard for the other while growing more and more detached from their spouses.

Soon Wasir began pressuring Ese to leave Sutekh to be with him. He was growing tired of sneaking around like a criminal. Besides that, he believed that with his newfound status as the most revered king of Alkebulan he deserved a queen of her stature by his side and he felt that Nebet just wasn't cutting it. Nebet just wasn't up to his standards anymore and it was time for him to replace her with a queen who was more on his level.

Meanwhile, Nebet had just bore a son for Wasir, which was of no consequence to him as it in no way changed his decision to leave her for her sister. He needed a change and as king he would ultimately get what he wanted.

However, Wasir's disloyalty impacted the world in a way that went well beyond him. He started a trend where queens were treated like changes of clothing. It was a trend that would go on to plague the divine ones for generations to come. In fact, it was the adulterous act of Wasir and Ese that would go on to devastate the entire existence of the divine ones taking them to a low that would be near impossible for them to resurrect from and dealing them a blow from which they would never be able to recover.

As time went on both Sutekh and Nebet began to suspect that something was amidst with their spouses. Eventually, their misery with their relationships drove them both to doing a little detective work to find out just what it was. It was Sutekh who was the first to reveal the truth and from there all hell broke lose.

12

It was their carelessness that ultimately made them get caught. Over time, Ese and Wasir got sloppy. Though Sutekh would have probably uncovered their deception as was his nature to do such things, Ese and Wasir became too remiss.

Sutekh was known throughout the universe as "the light bringer." He earned that title because he was the one who was strong enough to possess Re's light. However, it also meant that he had the power to shed light in the darkest of places. As a result, there was nothing that could be hidden from Sutekh because by possessing the light of Re he could see all things, which meant that he could see what others could not. That was why he was so knowledgeable. He possessed the knowledge of the entire universe.

Additionally, Sutekh, like Re was both a creator and a great destroyer. Thus, when he finally learned of Ese and Wasir's deception Sutekh

Black Man
was overcome with a rage that nothing in all of existence could control.

It happened one evening right after the hour of sunset that Sutekh put it all together. He was sitting in the heavens with Ese suffering through another deathly silent evening of absolute boredom. It had gotten to the point that he was on the verge of erupting.

Ese barely spoke to him anymore. More than that she didn't even try to take the least bit of interest in anything that had to do with Sutekh. He would try to discuss things that were going on in the cosmos with her only for her to reply nonchalantly with dead silence and a coldness that could freeze over the Arctic ten times. Sutekh was tired of trying to reach Ese who always seemed miles away.

As he watched her that evening he grew angry enough to erupt. Sutekh tried with everything in him to calm himself down enough to possibly lighten the mood. So he reminisced on a happier time. He remembered when he and Ese would enjoy one another's company talking for hours going from one subject to another. It seemed then that everything about him was of interest to her. Though as he looked at her he wondered if any of it was ever real. He always had a suspicion that she wasn't totally happy with him, but he would always clear such thoughts from his mind. Yet, with everything in him he wanted to believe that he could still somehow satisfy Ese.

Though despite his efforts Ese always managed to make Sutekh feel that he was just not good enough. Indirectly she belittled him and secretly she despised him. His mere touch soon made her cringe in disgust. The sight of him repulsed her. Gradually, Ese grew to wish that she had never chosen Sutekh. In her mind, she deserved a life with Wasir and being with Sutekh was simply her settling for much less than she deserved.

Ese felt that all that Sutekh had ever given her was a life of boredom with all of his endless babbling about all of the problems of the universe. She felt that he was too focused on problems and not focused enough on the beauty of life. When she was with Wasir he allowed her to see the endless possibilities in life. He made her feel special and beautiful. Besides that she loved him in a way that she had never loved Sutekh. It was a deeper love, a love that penetrated the very depths of her.

As she sat in silence with Sutekh she thought that perhaps the time had come for her to tell him that she was leaving. It was as good a time as any so she went for it.

Black Man

"I don't want to do this anymore. I'm just not happy and I know you're not either," Ese said coldly.

"So that's it. Just like that. You're done. You don't even want to try," Sutekh responded.

"We *have* tried. In fact, we've tried for a long time now and it just hasn't worked," Ese answered.

"No, *I've* tried. *You've* given up. You gave up a long time ago and because of that we never stood a chance," Sutekh said trying his best to maintain his composure. Then he paused and asked candidly, "So who is it? I know there's someone else. I saw when it happened. I noticed the change in you. So who is is?" Sutekh inquired.

Without pause or delay in responding Ese said curtly, "Hmmph funny you should ask. You're going to find out anyway so I might as well tell you. It's Wasir. It's your brother. He loves me and I love him and the truth is I've always loved him more. I guess I chose you because you were the strongest one and I admired your strength. Though I guess in the end that just wasn't enough."

Ese surprised even herself with how well she just blurted it all out and she was relieved to finally have it all out in the open. She was tired of sneaking around like some criminal.

Black Man

Meanwhile, Sutekh was taken aback by Ese's smug calmness and because of it he knew that she was telling the truth and that she *had* been with Wasir. She had apparently been with him for some time because she exuded his same arrogance.

Instantly, Sutekh's shock turned to the most intense rage Ese had ever seen. His fury could be felt throughout both the heavens and the underworld. Then before Ese could even process what was happening, Sutekh was gone. He had transported himself down to earth to confront Wasir.

"Hmmm I didn't expect to see you here. What brings you down from the heavens brother?" Wasir asked Sutekh as he was fading in and surprisingly relaxed.

"Well I thought it'd been awhile since I checked in on things down here. Wanted to see how much progress you've made. I hear you're the big man in town these days," Sutekh said sarcastically.

"Well I guess that may be true. The people do tend to say that about me," Wasir said arrogantly. Cloaked in his own narcissism he couldn't help but admire himself in all of his self-perceived grandeur.

Black Man

It took everything in Sutekh to keep his cool until the time was right to strike. He was baiting Wasir and he was not yet ready to strike.

Just as Wasir felt justified in sleeping with Sutekh's wife because he believed that he in some way had been wronged by Sutekh, Sutekh felt justified in killing his brother for sleeping with his wife because of his arrogance. So Sutekh waited for Wasir to display that oh familiar cloak of cynicism about having committed what was the ultimate act of betrayal.

13

Just then it happened. As expected, Wasir's egotism came shining through.

"Yes *everyone* loves me. By the way, you know I saw Ese not too long ago. She's been down here helping out quite a lot actually," Wasir gloated.

It was all that Sutekh needed as an invitation to strike. Wasir's cockiness was an illness that had to be dealt with and Sutekh had just the cure. Within an instant Sutekh dealt Wasir the deadliest of blows. With his brute strength and razor-sharp fingers Sutekh, with the mere wave of his hand sliced Wasir up into 42 pieces. Then still enraged, he ran about grumbling and scattering Wasir's remains all across the galaxy. Afterwards, once he had felt some vindication and was able to calm himself back down Sutekh returned to the heavens just as calmly as he had arrived to earth without saying a single word to Ese.

The death of Wasir could be felt all across the universe. Ese seemed most affected by his death as she arrived on earth soon after profusely crying the tears of a million storms. She felt a pain like no other and the only one that could comfort her was her sister Nebet.

It was strange, but somehow, despite her anger, Nebet understood Ese's pain and because of her undying love for her sister she offered her comfort. Later the two sisters agreed to work together to locate the remains of Wasir so that they could use Nebet's magic to put him back together again.

Ese desperately wanted Wasir back and though Ese's foulness for sleeping around with Nebet's husband was bad enough to stink up a galaxy, the power of the bond of their sisterhood superseded Nebet's anger at Ese's betrayal. So together they both grieved as they searched.

After some time had passed and using a lot of magic the sisters located every piece of Wasir's body with the exception of the phallus. Ese continued to search for it, but to no avail. Finally she gave up and used her magic to create one.

Ese wanted what she had never had, which was a child. However she didn't want the child of Sutekh. She wanted Wasir's child so she used the magically created phallus to impregnate herself. However as fate would have it things did not go

Black Man

according to her plans. Ese was pregnant, but contrary to her beliefs it was not the child of Wasir.

The identity of the child's father went on to become yet another of Ese's deep, dark secrets. She quietly tucked it away and told the world that she bore the son of Wasir. Consequently, Ese's son, Har, grew to bare a reputation of greatness under the legacy of Wasir.

However, more importantly, because Sutekh had murdered who Har thought was his father Har was dead set on avenging his father's death. Har grew up consumed with vengeance and thus he spent all of his time plotting his redress. This began a war that would go on for centuries. It was a war that further widened the wedge between the divine ones.

Some sided with Sutekh, but most sided with Har. They sympathized with him as they too missed Wasir. Since his death things hadn't been the same. Great leaders followed, but the divine ones had convinced themselves that there had been none greater than Wasir. So they too felt Har's pain and understood his need for vindication.

Finally, Har was ready to attack Sutekh. Yet, when he did as fortified as Har was made by his anger he still was not strong enough to defeat Sutekh. Not only did Sutekh supercede Har in strength, but he was also older and wiser, which made him quite the challenging adversary.

Ese tried to lend her son assistance, but it was to no avail. Often Har would not heed Ese's advice as he believed her judgement was compromised since Sutekh was her husband.

Meanwhile, Ese was finding that it was becoming increasingly more difficult to continue on keeping the true identity of Har's father a secret. Not being able to tell anyone was beginning to eat her up inside. In fact, a lot of what Ese had done in her not so distant past was beginning to eat away at her.

Ese began to spend a lot of time pondering the mistakes that she had made and she became remorseful. She even reached out to Sutekh to apologize for how she had wronged him. He forgave her, but refused to take her back. She had betrayed him in a way that he could not bear to relive again, which he did every time he looked at Ese.

Realizing that it was her actions that had set all the wheels in motion to starting the war between Har and Sutekh, Ese began to feel torn. She tried several times to talk Har out of continuing to fight Sutekh as it was going nowhere and solving nothing. She knew even though what she did had greatly angered Sutekh, in each battle he was taking it easy on Har for her sake. So she knew that Sutekh would never actually hurt Har permanently. Ese also knew that if Sutekh intended to defeat Har he would have. Thus, she tried to convince Har that avenging his father's death was not about a physical defeat of Sutekh. She explained to Har that it was instead about a mental conquest. She told Har that the true battle was within himself.

It was a universal law that was most commonly known as the law of mentalism. The law of mentalism posited that the All is the mind. Thus, Ese explained to Har that the war that he was fighting against Sutekh represented the war that was going on within him. She advised him that he was going about defeating Sutekh all wrong. It was he who was his own enemy, thus his true enemy was the enemy within. Therefore, he needed to deal with whatever issues were plaguing him.

Har did not want to hear any of Ese's babbling and after the second time Ese approached him with such advice Har actually began to aggressively attack his own mother. He accused her of betraying his father by siding with his killer. Har became enraged with Ese displaying a temper reminiscent of Sutekh.

One day Sutekh witnessed that same rage in Har for himself. It startled him so much that it

Black Man

moved him to question Ese concerning the identity of Har's father. After seeing the display of Har's rage he suspected that Ese had lied about Wasir being the father. Sutekh began to believe that *he* was Har's father. So day while they were both in the heavens he decided to ask Ese straight out.

"Who is Har's father? You say it is Wasir, but he carries traits nothing like my brother and I knew him better than anyone. So the truth, NOW!" Sutekh roared.

Taken aback by the question, Ese was momentarily frozen in shock. She wondered how Sutekh found out. Looking at her Sutekh knew that he was right. He didn't need to hear Ese say the words aloud. Her face said it all. He couldn't believe that again she had betrayed him. It was an even more foul betrayal than the first.

"I am ashamed of what I have done. This was a deception of the worst kind," Ese said bowing her head in shame.

Sutekh for millenniums had so longed for a child, a son, but Ese would always make up some excuse for why it wasn't a good idea. It was either that the time was not right or that she had not yet prepared her body. Then when she ran out of excuses she convinced Sutekh that he was barren and that not even her magic could cure him. Though Sutekh knew better than to believe that story as he was a God, which meant that he had the power to create whatever he wanted, including a child. Besides that, not only were the Gods fertile, but the abundance of the universe was always accessible to them upon a mere command.

Once again enraged Sutekh struck Ese a look of utter disgust. He couldn't believe that she had again deceived him. Sutekh wondered how he could have so many times allowed Ese to manipulate him. He also wondered why time after time she felt the need to inflict so much pain upon him. What had he done to her to deserve such treatment? As far as he was concerned all that he had ever done was love her. He began to think that perhaps that was the problem.

As he continued to ponder the situation he concluded that Ese was one who would never be satisfied. Nothing would have ever been enough for her and more than anything, in her eyes Sutekh would never be a worthy companion.

Yet, despite the utter rage that he was feeling towards Ese after what she had done, Sutekh was surprisingly calm when he looked at Ese and simply replied, "Where is my son now?"

Ese had prepared for the worst. She knew all too well of Sutekh's temper and a betrayal of this magnitude was sure to send him over the edge. She didn't buy the eery sense of calm that Sutekh

Black Man

displayed. Nonetheless, she decided to tell Sutekh where Har was because she knew that truth was what she owed him.

  Without saying another word to Ese and within an instant later Sutekh went to find Har. Sutekh wanted to address Har father to son. Har had the right to know the true identity of his father and Sutekh had the right to have his son know that he was his father. As it was they had both been cheated out of many years as father and son and for the opportunity to build a relationship. So Sutekh made his way to Har anxious to change the dynamics of their relationship.

14

Har was up in the mountains deep in meditation when Sutekh found him. Sutekh was actually surprised to find him engaged in such an activity as it was often one of the things that he too did to calm himself down and get himself refocused on more important matters at hand.

Har didn't seem surprised to see Sutekh there. Nor did he appear to show any fear for having been caught off guard.

"Hello Har," Sutekh greeted, "You should know that I come in peace. I don't want to fight you anymore."

"Oh is that a fact. Well you know what uncle? It just so happens that I'm done fighting you also. I've had an epiphany and I realized that I don't need to fight you anymore," Har answered.

"Yeah I know meditation can certainly have that effect. Well I'm glad to hear that, but I'm actually here to discuss another matter with you," Sutekh said making it a point to tread lightly.

Black Man

Since things were finally peaceful between them Sutekh didn't want to jeopardize it by breaking the big news too abruptly. So he waited patiently until he felt the time was right for the big disclosure.

"There's something that you should know Har. I know a bit about acting on rage and not thinking. I learned a long time ago that you have to choose your battles. You also have to find a way to stay balanced so that you don't find yourself spiraling out of control. Most importantly what I also learned is that the true enemy is within. I've unjustly waged more wars than I care to admit. In the end I had to realize that I was the source of my own frustration. It was something in me that I saw in someone else that caused me to get upset. Once I dealt with that the war ended and I was then victorious," Sutekh advised.

"Yeah I get that, sort of. So why are you telling me all of this?" Har asked.

"Well I guess it's because I see that there is a connection between us. It's been that same connection that has caused us to be at odds. I guess you could say that it's opened my eyes to some things," Sutekh explained.

"Why are you being so mysterious? Is there something that you need to say to me? If so, just say it. I was kind of busy and I'd like to get back to what I was doing," Har said coldly.

Black Man

"You are definitely your mother's child," Sutekh said looking at Har shaking his head before continuing.

"Well there's no easy way to say what I have to say. I'm just trying to be considerate of the sensitivity of the matter. But anyway, I guess there's no real easy way to do this so I'll just go ahead and tell you..." Sutekh began.

Just as he was about tell Har who his father was Ese appeared. It was as if she sensed that her big secret was just about to be disclosed and was making an attempt to stop it. Pleading with Sutekh with her eyes she revealed that she was in fact coming to stop him from telling Har.

After Sutekh left all of it started to really sink in for Ese and she began to see the true ramifications of what the revelation of this secret would do to her. Her whole existence would be turned upside down. She would lose everything, namely everyone's respect. Most importantly, she would lose Har. Ese just knew that if Sutekh told Har the truth about what she had done, he would never forgive her and neither would Nebet. It was the worst betrayal imaginable for a child to have to endure and Ese did not want to be the parent to do such a thing.

Ese's nerves were on pins and needles as she pled regretfully with her eyes. Her mind was racing as she envisioned all the possible ways the whole thing could play out. She didn't know if Har would react like his father with unimaginable rage or if he'd be more like her and be very cold and never speak to her again. Either way she saw it playing out the end result wouldn't be good for her.

Nonetheless, ignoring Ese's pathetic expression Sutekh continued. He didn't care about what Ese wanted. He figured that she certainly didn't care anything about how he felt when she committed one betrayal after another having an affair with his brother then lying about the identity of his child. Besides that he was maxed out on being so loving and considerate of her feelings when she could have cared less about him or his feelings. So Sutekh focused his attention back onto Har set on telling him the truth and letting the chips fall where they may.

"Har, I came here to tell you something. Something that you have the right to know," Sutekh said before pausing to gauge Har's response.

"Oh yeah and what is that?" Har replied blankly and seemingly still uninterested.

"Your father is not who you think it is. Yet I suspect that you may already know that, which is why you're here. I believe that you did some introspective digging and discovered that for yourself. I know that once you thought about it you

Black Man

saw that you shared absolutely nothing in common with Wasir. He's always been bound to the underworld while you've always taken to the skies. His other attributes were more likened to that of humanity and the savage race while yours were more Godly. Then most apparently, your mother is my wife, which I'm sure made you beg the question of whether I was in fact your father? Well, I am," Sutekh said as his last words echoed in Ese's ears sending a pang of pain straight through the depths of her heart as she looked over at Har apologetically.

Ese was riddled with shame as she kept hearing the last few words that Sutekh had said echo over and over again in her head. Meanwhile, Har looked over at her with the most hurt look on his face. Ese had never seen Har look that way.

However, she decided not to deny the truth that Sutekh had just revealed as it was finally *all* out and on the table. Besides that, she briefly felt relieved. Contrary to what she felt just moments earlier, she was finally prepared to admit to herself that she was tired of carrying the burden of so big a lie around. So essentially what Sutekh had just done was a welcomed relief.

So instead of denying anything or running away Ese drew on some courage, looked Har in the eye and finally faced her worst fear. It was time and she was tired of running from what was inevitably bound to be her doom. Ese had no idea how Har would respond. He had attacked her in the past for siding with Sutekh so she did not know what to expect. Though Ese was ready to accept responsibility for what she had done, she was not ready to deal with the prospect of possibly losing her son forever as she truly didn't know whether he'd ever speak to her again.

Har was eerily calm as both Ese and Sutekh awaited his response to the revelation. In the past it usually took way less to make him explode so what they were observing puzzled them both. Har merely continued to sit in his meditative posture with the most uncanny look of calm anyone had ever witnessed in him.

For Har the revelation was the end of the battle that had been raging within him for far too long. The calm that Sutekh and Ese observed was a reflection of the calm that truth had manifested within him.

As Har looked at Ese who had caused so many around her including herself so much pain all for the sake of her own self interest he realized, in that moment, the valuable lesson in it all.

He learned of the true meaning of love. He learned that true love is giving and receiving seeking nothing in return, which Ese knew nothing of. Instead, Ese was always warring against love. Not once did she love without the prospect of there being something in it for her. She initially 'loved' Sutekh because of his strength, which gave her a sense of strength. Yet she never *gave* in that relationship. Then she 'loved' Wasir because she wanted to feel something that she didn't feel with Sutekh. Yet all she gave Wasir in exchange was an illusion, which meant that essentially she had not *given* anything.

Besides that it was Ese who was losing the war raging within herself. She did so by continuing to seek out love outside of herself. Then, when she realized that such a thing did not exist she became a Goddess scorned, striking out against all of those closest to her. She was later so blinded by her own self-interest in this quest that she didn't care who she hurt in the process of trying to obtain it.

So it was easy for her to betray the sanctity of her marriage and place the blame on her husband. It was easy for her to betray the trust of her sister by having an affair with her husband. Then it was easy for her to find justification for lying to her son about the identity of his father.

Seeking love outside of herself made Ese cold and baseless. Thus, the war raging inside of her had to do with her needing to establish love within. She needed to ground herself in that love

Black Man
and in doing so it would not have been so easy for her to succumb to the whims of her emotions, which did nothing but wreak havoc in her life.

    Har looked at his mother and her look of shame and he realized that her shame was an illness. It was an illness that, with his prophetic ability, he could see would go on to germinate and replay itself in Goddesses over and over again for generations to come. Goddesses would continue to seek love outside of themselves and never truly find it until they searched within. Thus, they would go on lashing out at the ones closest to them, all in the name of love.

15

Nigga sat in the courtroom reminiscing on a past life where he had too often been blindly led by what he *thought* was love. He saw how far from Godliness doing so had caused him to stray.

As he looked over on the side of the prosecutor's table where his third child's mother sat across from him staring at him coldly he thought about the impact of all the lies she had used to manipulate him, much like his mother had done. Often times she *and* his mother even teamed up against him.

It always angered Nigga to think about the loyalty between the women in his life that always seemed to cause him such suffering. No matter what any of them did to wrong him they would defend one another to the end. It was one of the main things that Nigga hated being the victim of.

As he looked around the courtroom Nigga saw what represented a legacy of sickness. It was a sickness so ruthless that it managed to transform Gods into the damned. Even worse, it was a disease that was of their own creation. Memories of how the disease infected them flooded Niggas mind as he sat in deep contemplation still gathering his thoughts about his closing statements.

Nigga remembered back when he was a small child, about 7 or 8 years old. He could remember it so clearly. His parents were still together and the year was around 1978. His parents were still quite young and they lived in a small two-bedroom apartment in Harlem. His father had just bought a 1973 Mercury Capri and Nigga was going with his dad to take it out for a spin. He relived the memory in slow motion and it felt like he and his dad had driven all over New York. It was a memory that forever stayed imprinted in his mind. He cherished those times with his dad because it seemed that just days later everything took a turn for the worst.

He didn't know what they were arguing about, but his parents had a huge blow out and the next thing Nigga knew his parents were yelling at one another and cursing each other out. His mother was throwing random objects at Nigga's father and moments later she got so enraged that she charged at him. Then like an automatic reflex Nigga's father had grabbed her by the arms and was holding her down. In that moment, in what

Black Man

seemed like the blink of an eye Nigga's *best* memory transformed into his *worst* nightmare.

Yet, the most memorable part of that day was that it was the last time Nigga ever saw his father. He'd occasionally spoken to him over the phone, but his mother made sure that Nigga's father never saw him again.

It wasn't until later that he learned that his parents were fighting about his father's infidelity. His father had been cheating on his mother and not only did he get caught, but he ended up getting the other woman pregnant.

Nigga's mother was devastated. Nigga remembered nights when she would cry herself to sleep and as the new man of the house he would do his best to console her. However, after that Nigga became the object of her disgust. Everything that she hated about Nigga's father became everything that she saw in Nigga and that she hated about the black man. Nigga became the source of her perpetual state of heartbreak.

Most of all, if he didn't learn anything else from her, what he *did* learn was that he was growing up to be *just like his father*. That was the phrase that Nigga heard for the rest of his life every time he did anything that was contrary to her liking, which was most things.

Black Man

It was Nigga's mother's way of getting some form of retribution for how Nigga's father had betrayed her. It was also her way of controlling Nigga. What Nigga's father had done to her was the ultimate betrayal and one that she was never able to get over. So Nigga was cursed to serve a life sentence for a crime that he didn't even commit. Yet, he paid dearly and the biggest price of all that he had to pay was never seeing his father again.

Over the years things got progressively worse between Nigga and his mother. Their relationship seemed irreparable. So when Nigga turned 15 he moved out on his own. Soon after he dropped out of school, eventually got a crappy job, which managed to be enough for him to rent a rundown room.

Though he had escaped the choke hold of his mother what he found was that when he went out into the world, he was still serving out his sentence for what his father had done. Nigga saw it as he went from one relationship to the next.

His first relationship was with a girl name Tonya. Tonya was a cute, petite light complexioned girl that Nigga had met one day while hanging out with some friends. She was walking by and immediately caught Nigga's eyes so he approached her, seemingly captured her interest as well, then after a couple of times hanging out they were a couple.

Tonya was what Nigga thought was the sweetest girl. In the beginning they got along pretty well and consequently he dated her for 3 years before they had their first child. It was a baby boy, whom Nigga named Elijah. When Elijah was born they were both only 19 years old and had not the first clue about parenting. Besides that neither of them had the maturity to take on the responsibility of a relationship, adulthood and a child. Therefore, as expected, it didn't take long before things fell apart.

In particular, it was Tonya who couldn't deal with the pressures of parenting. She began to feel as if she was suffocating. She wanted to enjoy her young adult life instead, doing all the fun things that young adults her age did like party, be carefree and hang out. Parenting was just too much for her as was a serious relationship. So most of the time she dropped their son off at her mother's so that she could go out and party. This angered Nigga and they would often get into heated arguments about it. Eventually one argument led to another, which led to a couple of fights which ultimately ended their relationship.

Once they parted ways, Tonya made it impossible for Nigga to see his son. Even though

Black Man

she didn't want the responsibility of raising Elijah out of spite she didn't want Nigga to either. She didn't want him to experience any of the joys of fatherhood that she knew he would undoubtedly do given how close he was to his son.

Nigga pled with Tonya on numerous occasions to just give him custody of their son and let him raise him, but she refused. Then the more he pled, the more vindictive she became. Tonya discovered that she could use Elijah as a weapon against Nigga. So she proceeded to drag Nigga through what turned out to be the most horror-filled tour of the New York child support system that any man had ever lived through.

Out of all the child support jurisdictions in the United States, New York was by far the worst. It was the black man's death sentence because after being brought into it he would never escape. Beyond that, like the vampire it was, it would bleed him dry. He may as well have been sentenced to do time at Riker's Island prison, which some actually were!

Consequently, Tonya's wrath was just the first of many with each one being ten times worse than the one before. Nigga could not figure out what he'd ever done to anger black woman so. It was as if he had been chosen to pay for the sins of

Black Man
a million brothahs and he simply could not understand why.

All he wanted more than anything was to raise his children. Yet, time after time all the black woman did was wield his children as weapons against him. To her he was and would forever be enemy number 1, not the white man who used trickery to manipulate her, not her own deadbeat father, not the government who encouraged her to maintain an antagonistic relationship with her children's fathers in exchange for the bread crumbs that were public welfare benefits, and not the brothahs who came after Nigga who lacked any respect for her as a queen.

Rather it was Nigga who they viewed as the sole source of her pain, life failures and all things evil in the world. Nigga who wanted nothing more than to be a father to his children, to be respected as a man, to be a source of strength in his community and to be afforded the freedom to be in control of his life.

Then, besides the black woman, Nigga grew to hate how easily a judge could dictate every aspect of his life. Once Tonya entered him into the child support system merely at the strike of a gavel a judge had determined that Nigga would not be granted the opportunity to be a father to his children. The judge had also determined how much

Black Man

money Nigga needed in order to live out what he, as the judge, deemed a satisfactory life. The judge determined the type of lifestyle Nigga would be afforded as well as the type of career he would pursue. It was a level of control that was debilitating to Nigga's confidence as a man.

Meanwhile, though the judge was Nigga's worse nightmare, for the black woman the judge was her her protector, the head of her household, the father who knew what was best for her family, the man that she honored and ultimately he was everything that the black man was not. The judge was her source of empowerment. The judge was her weapon of choice and she wielded him like a deadly weapon.

It was a reality that would go on to impact the lives of both black men, black women and children for generations to come. The effects would be catastrophic because it was the thing that forever changed the dynamics of the black community at large.

It seemed that no one could ever quite come up with the direct cause nor did anyone have a solution. Insead everyone continued to fight, which continued to divide producing a generation of children who were deeply troubled, distrustful, abandoned and in many cases unloved.

Black Man

16

Tonya's attack against Nigga was followed by JeJuan who had chosen a somewhat different weapon of choice to use against Nigga. JeJaun was the cousin of one of Nigga's friends. He'd met her at one of their family cookouts. JeJaun, like Tonya started out as being a very sweet girl. She was also very attractive having thickness in all the right places, making Nigga the envy of all of his male peers.

JeJaun was a very outgoing girl. She was educated, had an honorable career as a teacher and good family values, which Nigga liked most of all. He was with JeJuan for five years. During the course of that time they had two children together, twin daughters Aisha and Amaya, who absolutely adored Nigga. Unlike Tonya, JeJaun was quite the nurturing type and was a very good mother to their daughters.

JeJuan had one major complaint about

Black Man

Nigga, which was that he did not worship her god. JeJaun was a devout Christian and she hated that Nigga did not share her zeal for the lord. Though JeJaun knew when she hooked up with Nigga that he was not the religious type, she figured that in time she could convert him and so she proceeded to pursue the relationship despite her misgivings about his spirituality.

Yet the years went by and Nigga was just as anti-religious as he was when she met him. Eventually, JeJaun grew tired of *living in sin* with Nigga as he had still not married her and seemingly had no plans to.

JeJaun became angry and bitter as the years went by feeling guilty for being with a man that did not share her religious beliefs and who would not, after five years and two children, marry her. So in time, secretly JeJaun began to harbor a great disdain for Nigga. Eventually, the very sight of him repulsed her. Then later she became irritated by all of his flaws, some that only she seemed to see.

Besides that, in JeJaun's eyes, unlike her pastor, Nigga was lazy and not nearly outgoing enough. He didn't have big enough aspirations and he simply lacked direction and focus. She also didn't like that he taught their children of *his* irreverent spiritual beliefs, which were quite contrary

Black Man

to her own. JeJaun intended to raise their children as good, wholesome, god-fearing, Christian girls. She'd die before she saw them grow to become the heretics that Nigga was teaching them to be. So it was that which was the straw that broke the camel's back for JeJaun.

So one Sunday when JeJaun came home from church she told Nigga that the lord had told her that she needed to ask him to leave. She told Nigga that he was taking her on a wayward path and causing her to stray from her god. She also told Nigga that he was evil and that she wanted no parts of his wicked ways.

Nigga left, but told JeJaun that she would not keep him from his kids nor would she prevent him from being an influence in their life. Consequently, what Nigga said had absolutely no impact on JeJaun, because like Tonya she wielded child support like a samurai sword keeping him at bay and away from his children. It obliterated Nigga's heart as he was very close to his children. Then if that wasn't bad enough she joined forces with his mother launching one attack after another on him.

One would have thought that JeJaun and Nigga's mother were partners in crime. They defended one another to the end and Nigga's mother co-signed everything that JeJaun either said

Black Man
or did. As far as Nigga's mother was concerned JeJaun could do no wrong and it was Nigga who needed to get himself together. In her eyes he would always be nothing more than a disappointment just like his father. Nigga knew that both of them were a lost cause as they were both too caught up in their own self-inflicted abuse and so he gave up the fight against them and moved on.

Next, there was Shana, who was the mother of Nigga's youngest child, a boy named K'eon. Nigga and Shana were never actually in a relationship. In fact, their relationship was in large part the source of much of the controversy between Nigga, JeJaun and Nigga's mother.

Nigga had impregnated Shana while he was still with JeJaun. For JeJaun, it was yet another reason why she broke things off with him, why the lord told her to make him leave and why Nigga's mother sided with her. For Nigga's mother it was a cruel reminder of what Nigga's father had done to her. What Nigga had done to JeJaun was like deja vu and all she saw was his father's betrayal all over again.

Nigga knew that there was no justification for what he had done with Shana. He knew that if nothing else he should have protected himself to avoid having another child, especially with someone he wasn't even in a relationship with and had no intentions on being with. He didn't even have a good explanation for doing what he had done. Sure he and JeJaun had differing spiritual views, but that was the case when they met.

Nigga knew that cheating on JeJaun was not the solution to any of their problems. Besides that, given that they were already having so many problems he knew that he had no right to bring yet another person into the mix. JeJaun was nurturing, loyal and loving despite her spiritual hang-ups and in no way deserved a betrayal of that magnitude. He felt bad for having again allowed his family to be split up and having to again lose children because of it devastated him. JeJaun was definitely the one that Nigga knew he treated unjustly.

Soon enough he realized that in doing so all he had managed to do was land himself right back in child support court again facing yet another child-support threatening bandit, Shana. However, Shana was more vicious than both of his other children's mothers put together. Shana was methodical and clever and she knew the New York child support and public welfare systems like the back of her hand. It seemed she'd gotten a phD in it. She made the system work for her in ways that no other woman could.

Shana worked in a law firm as a paralegal and so she had access to resources that neither of

Nigga's other children's mothers had. In fact, the attorney that had represented her in prior trials was one of the lawyers from the firm she worked for and he was one of the best. In addition to that Shana carried in her purse of tricks the wrath of a woman who had been rejected. Because of that she did everything in her power to make Nigga's life a living hell.

She had pressed phone harassment and assault charges against him. She had gotten restraining orders against him. She even started sleeping with a brothah who Nigga thought was one of his good friends then used him to testify against Nigga in court. Then if that wasn't bad enough, Shana did the unthinkable, she had Nigga charged with criminal child support, which was what he was presently in court for and facing a possible prison sentence of up to 4 years and a $5000 fine.

Shana was a heartbroken woman scorned all because she had been the other women in Nigga's life. For her what made it worse was that even when the relationship between he and JeJuan ended he still chose not to be with her. So she was bitter and out for blood.

Out of the three, Shana was probably the most attractive of all of Nigga's children's mothers. She looked like a model. Besides that she was the most accomplished. She had the most going for her and in her opinion she was every man's dream. To top it off she was the down girl who understood her man and didn't mind being an ear about the problems he was having at home. She could keep their secret and to her that meant that she was loyal. In Shana's mind this was her ticket in. It was how she planned to get the top spot despite the fact that she told Nigga that she was okay being *the other woman*. Secretly, she was planning and dreaming about being Nigga's number one and only.

However, Nigga's perception of Shana was very different from hers. She was literally the other woman and he had no intentions of making her anything else. Plus, even if he *was* single, to him Shana was the woman that really didn't even need a man. She was well taken care of all on her own. Besides that at the time that he met her, he was already in a relationship with someone that he cared about. He was more than open with Shana about his intentions and so for him there were no mixed signals sent and he didn't understand why she was tripping.

The only reason that he got involved with Shana was because he became dissatisfied with his relationship with JeJaun. However, it was a mistake that he would regret for the rest of his life

Black Man

because out of them all Shana was the most ruthless.

Later on Nigga even found out that Shana had used her legal resources to join forces with Tonya to build her case against him. It was clear to Nigga that Shana would stop at nothing to make his suffering painstakingly tortuous and long-lasting. So she proceeded to make the rest of his days a living hell for what he had done to her and for that Nigga would always have regrets.

Yet as he sat across from Shana in the courtroom watching her pompous expression there was no doubt in his mind that he was at a turning point in his life. Despite all of his poor judgement, bad decisions, undying love for his children, battles with his mother and the internal war that was brewing inside he knew with everything in him that the time had finally come for him to change his story for the better. He looked across the room at Shana and he knew that the time had come for his transformation back into the God.

17

While many memories of his life flashed through his mind Nigga couldn't help but wonder why him? Why had he been plagued with so much turmoil all throughout his life? Was he so bad a person that he deserved it?

For the most part Nigga had been quite an honorable man. Sure he had made his fair share of bad judgement calls, but who hadn't. He didn't deserve to be demonized for it. Yet there he sat in a courtroom full of people who looked at him like he was the devil incarnate. Momentarily, he began to think, maybe he was.

It wouldn't the first time that Nigga thought such thoughts nor would it be the last. Such thoughts were what led Nigga to venture deep into the recesses of his mind to investigate who he was and why such things were happening to him. He figured he must have been somebody great because there were a lot of people that went through a lot of trouble to make his existence difficult.

At times it seemed as if the universal forces were all conspiring against him. For starters, he couldn't figure out why it was that nothing seemed to work in his favor. The more he tried the more he failed and for the life of him Nigga could not figure out why.

He only wanted to be able to take care of his children, play an active role in raising them, create economic stability for himself, be in control of his life and finally realize some success. He just wanted to feel a sense of satisfaction and every time he seemed to be on the path to doing just that forces rose up against him derailing his plans.

After several cycles of this Nigga supposed that it was all happening to make him stronger. Then he wondered how much stronger he needed to be and for what? Was there some huge event destined to occur in his life that required him to have some type of superhuman strength? Did he have some higher purpose? Did the universe have some great plan in store for him?

None of it made any sense to Nigga and he just wanted to know when it was finally going to be his chance to experience some happiness and success. Most importantly, he wanted to know

Black Man

when would *he* be given the opportunity to experience true love.

The only person that he remembered having felt true love from was his father. His father's love could be felt in his very essence. Nigga and his father were the best of friends. Time spent with his father was also the closest thing to happiness Nigga had ever experienced.

He could never understand why his mother had taken his father away. Secretly, he hated her for that. In fact, whenever he was having an honest moment with himself he knew that the fact was that he hated his mother for what she'd taken from him as much as she hated his father for betraying her trust.

Ironically, as a result, Nigga, like his mother, spent his life getting back at her through his treatment of other women the same way that his mother got back at Nigga's father through her treatment of him. Like his mother, Nigga often had no respect for women. He never allowed them to truly get close to him always being sure to maintain a safe emotional distance. He had a difficult time professing his love for them much like his mother who never told him she loved him. All she told him was how much of a failure he would be as a man *just like his father.* So ultimately, Nigga found it very difficult to even love a woman and doubted that he actually had ever done so.

Though he was in no way confused about his sexual identity, as a result he consequently had more love for his male peers, particularly his best friend Sha, than he ever had for any woman he'd been involved with. Nigga and Sha had pretty much grown up together and had been friends for over two decades. In Sha Nigga confided and shared all of his secrets. Nigga built and shared his dreams with Sha. Nigga had the highest degree of honor, loyalty and respect for Sha. Sha was his co-pilot in life. He was Nigga's backbone. When anything happened it was Sha who Nigga called on. Sha was the first and last person that Nigga spoke to everyday. In Nigga's eyes Sha was the only one who truly understood him. Sha knew him better than even his own mother. Sha had been with him through thick and thin. Sha had been Nigga's biggest support. As a result, Nigga was committed to Sha for life and it was a level of commitment that he had never truly given any woman.

On the other hand, while there were many other brothahs who had shared this same type of loving relationship with the women in their life, Nigga had never experienced such a relationship with *any* woman whom he'd ever been with. At the

Black Man

same time he never even tried to open himself up to the prospect of doing so.

To Nigga women only represented all that was wrong in the world. To him relationships with them represented pain, not love and companionship. In his mind, he could get that only from Sha and so he resolved to not look for it elsewhere. He saw women as mere objects who were there only to facilitate his needs. In fact, this were a part of his spiritual beliefs and in large part the source of contention during many of his debates about spirituality with JeJaun.

Eventually, Nigga developed the victim's psychology about his life circumstances, particularly with regards to black women. So in his mind he became every black woman's target. It was the black woman who had obliterated him into a thousand pieces. Thus he had sentenced himself to a lifetime of suffering as he struggled to put the pieces of himself back together again. In his mind every black woman hated him. He saw it as being her nature to do so. As far as he was concerned all black women knew how to be was disloyal, sneaky, manipulative, and underhanded.

Nigga began to secretly view all things feminine as bad and so he did everything in his power to align himself with all things masculine. After all, the Gods were a masculine energy that

Black Man

were superior to all and he considered himself as one among the Gods. The Gods were the All in All, the only, the alpha, the supreme, the creator. There was no Goddess, no polarity to balance the God out. There was no opposite to whom he was magnetically attracted to. There was only him alone in his universe.

Nigga was a fallen God in resistance and at war with…..himself and didn't even know it. He mistakenly thought that his enemies were all the forces outside of himself such as his mother, every black woman who had ever wronged him, the court system, the government, his job and an endless list of others. However, when he finally had an honest moment with himself that day in the courtroom it hit him like a ton of bricks! He finally realized what the source of his problems had been all along. It was him!!! It was he who had been the worst of his enemies.

He realized that just as his own mother harbored certain resentments toward him, as a result he too had done the same to the black woman in several of his relationships, which was what led to their counterattacks. His emotional distance, disregard for her greatness, absence of loving sentiments, lack of support were all perceived as attacks against her. As a black woman it was her nature to desire to receive such

Black Man

things from Nigga, who she viewed as her king, her God, her All, her Supreme. Thus, when she didn't she grew angry and she waged war against him.

Nigga finally saw that though he'd always focused on the fact that many of the women he dealt with had many unresolved issues with their father, he too had many unresolved issues with his mother, which, like them, he had taken into his own relationships.

In relationships, Nigga had always maintained a safe distance from them in the same way that he had done with his mother. Perhaps it was her secrecy that discouraged him from being close to her or maybe it was her rejection of him that caused him to pull away. Whatever the case, Nigga knew that his unresolved issues with his mother were playing themselves out over and over again in his relationships and he realized that the time had come for him to resolve those issues once and for all. He was tired of carrying around the burden of them. Besides that he wanted to understand them so that he could grow from them.

It was a part of him. It was a part of his past that he desperately needed to make sense of. Nigga knew that once he did he would unlock the keys to his purpose, which he knew extended far beyond his fathering children and living a life of unfulfilled dreams.

Black Man

Then beyond his issues with the black woman Nigga also realized that it wasn't the court's fault they he had chosen to father all of those children at a time that he was not yet economically secure enough to support. Nor was it his job's fault that he found himself doing work that made him feel unfulfilled. Finally, having come full circle Nigga realized that it wasn't the fault of the black women with whom he had relationships that he was not able to truly love them. Nigga realized that there was a part of himself that he had to come to accept and love and that was the part that died when his father left.

Not even with all of his studying of the high spiritual sciences was Nigga able to resolve that very human issue. It was a human issue that needed to be resolved on a human level before Nigga could transform back into the God that he was destined to once again realize within. It was the human issue that had Nigga crippled, battered and confused and in a perpetual state of complacency that had ultimately led him down the road to nowhere. It was the human issue that was Nigga's greatest fear, a fear that he would then have to face that day in the courtroom for all the world to see.

As these thoughts raced through Nigga's mind he, without thinking, slowly and confidently

Black Man
rose up from his seat finally prepared to give his closing statements.

18

Then just before he uttered his first word Nigga saw flash before him all the ways that he had played and replayed out the same story of jealousy, vengeance, self-hatred, anger and internal warfare that he had when he knew himself to be a God. He had done the same thing lifetime after lifetime after lifetime. Seeing it flash before him he felt like a hamster on a running wheel and he had finally grown tired of doing all that running and going nowhere. It was finally time for him to face his enemy so he began....

"I've been here many times," Nigga said before pausing. "Each time is the same. I sit here in defense of myself, you the judges sit there with your judgements of me and you try, convict and sentence me before I even present my case. Each time, like today, I successfully disprove all that the

Black Man

prosecution presents as evidence against me. Yet the outcome is always the same. The court rules that I am the monster that has done nothing but invoke pain and suffering upon the women and children in my life making their lives a living hell and for that I should be severely punished and I agree. I have been a monster. I have been the monster, the demon, the evil, sinister force that has brought hardship into the world. In my own ignorance I have sabotaged every opportunity that has been presented to me to turn my situation around and I've blamed everyone else for it. I have lied, manipulated and cheated on the women who have tried to love me. I have used deception to get what I wanted often times playing the role of a loving man, but never truly feeling that way. I have allowed jealousy and anger to misguide me into some of the worst decisions of my life. Worst of all I have allowed myself to defy my own laws, now succumbing to such a base human level of this existence. I have reduced myself to this lowly, pathetic state rather than conducting myself as the God I know myself to be!"

  With that last statement every person in the courtroom looked at Nigga in shock. They were all frozen in disbelief. All around the room jaws dropped, eyes bugged out and eyebrows cringed. There were whispers about Nigga referring to

Black Man
himself as God. Then the judge struck the gavel and ordered everyone in the courtroom to settle down before instructing Nigga to please continue.

Nigga paused, slowly looked around the room making eye contact with the judge, the prosecutor, Shana, his mother and several strangers sitting in the pews.

He then took in a deep breath, parted his lips and said, "Meanwhile, as proven here today, which is what we are here to determine, I have shown undying love for my children, done the work to become a well-respected man of the community and exhibited great strength in facing the adversities that I have been faced with during this lifetime. I have worked tirelessly to meet the demands of caring for the material needs of my children as well as their mothers. I have done all of these things and therefore the only crimes that I am truly guilty of have been crimes committed against myself. So, yes, I am guilty of the crime of failing to love every aspect of myself as the creator of this place. By not loving the black woman beyond the pain of my actions against her I have in turn not loved myself as she is me by way of my creation. I am also guilty of the crime of allowing myself to succumb to my emotions making them my master. I Self Lord Am Master, thus such things should never have been allowed to happen in a reality of

Black Man

my creation. I am also guilty of the crime of forgetting who I am. I am the All-In-All, the Hidden One, the Light Bearer, the Supreme, the Naga!"

With that statement, everyone in the courtroom gasped with bugged out eyes as they whispered to one another in disbelief at what Nigga had just said. Again the judge had to strike to gavel to get the courtroom to settle down.

Once everyone had settled down Nigga continued while staring at the white judge intensely in the eyes. "Yet still, the crime that I am most guilty of that is the worst of all of my transgressions is that I have allowed the sickness that is you to manipulate, feed off of me, multiply and spread yourself, consuming every aspect of my existence. I have allowed YOU... this... this disease, this savage beast of a nightmare, this germ to geminate, possess and infect my seeds, my queen and my universe, turning them all against me. Yes, I, your Lord and Master, your God have done you quite a disservice. You are not meant to lead and it is my fault that you have been tasked with something that is beyond your infantile nature to do. So it is the guilt of my own crimes that has truly brought me here now. It is not of your doing that I am here and so for blaming you for that I do apologize and acknowledge my guilt."

Black Man

Then looking around at all the black women in the room Nigga said, "To you my queen I most humbly apologize for allowing myself to slip so far down into the humanity within myself that I let you down. I know that it was the sickness of that crime that has brought us both here. Down here is not where you deserve to be my love. You deserve to be up in the heavens, not down here in this lowly existence. Yet, though I have wronged you you have remained by my side. I know that it was my actions that made you cold. My excessive attention to so many other matters outside of my universe, my yoni-verse left you out in the cold, alone to fend for yourself. I know, as it is your warm, loving nature to desire such, you needed more of me at home."

Nigga then looked around the courtroom and made eye contact with all of the children and said, "And my seeds I owe YOU the biggest apology of all as you did nothing to deserve such a lowly display of me. You deserved to see me at my strongest. My stars you deserved to see me, your sun shine brightly for you. I will light the way for you now through this dark jungle so that you no longer have to guess your way home. This was a war that I alone was meant to fight. I never intended to bring my queen and my children into it. Now we are all fighting one another. You all don't belong in the

Black Man
battlefields. I was supposed to have you secured safely at home."

Finally, directing his attention back to the judge Nigga said, "So in closing I *am* guilty, but only of breaking laws that supercede your man-made ones. I have disproven every shred of evidence that the prosecution has presented here today. Thus, since I Self Lord Am Master and I alone have now made the unknown known I alone will issue my sentence. With that said it is my determination that my sentence has been served and I have paid my debt to my queen, my seeds and humanity."

For Nigga what he had just disclosed felt like the weight of a ton of boulders being lifted off of his back after having been lugged around for a lifetime. It felt like he'd finally located the light switch after having searched around for it in a crowded pitch black dark room for centuries. It felt like finally being able to breathe after having been forced to hold one's breath underwater for over 15 minutes. It felt like a cool oasis in the middle of the Sahara desert. It felt like being raised from the dead. It felt like being released from prison after serving an eighty-year sentence after having thought you'd never get out.

Black Man

19

The white judge looked at Nigga, his face turned flush, his eyebrows raised in anger, with pierced lips and narrowed eyes, then having raised the gavel up in his hand he looked at Nigga coldly and simply said, "For the charge of criminal non-support of child support this court hereby finds you guilty and I hereby sentence you to the fullest extent of the law to pay a fine of $5000 and serve 4 years in prison at Riker's Island Correctional Facility!" With that the judge then struck his gavel against the podium and immediately got up to exit the courtroom.

Everyone in the courtroom gasped loudly. They were all shocked that Nigga had to serve time after seeing the overwhelming amount of evidence that Nigga had presented in support of his innocence. More than that the prosecution had done an extremely poor job of owning their burden of proof in presenting evidence to prove Nigga's guilt. Often times it seemed they weren't even prepared, constantly making one excuse after another for why they couldn't back claims up with evidence.

Besides that the courtroom was filled with nothing but blacks who were all quite moved by Nigga's closing statements. So they were all very much in shock by the judge's ruling. Sure Nigga may have gone a bit far calling himself Lord and Master, but as he said he had disproven every shred of evidence brought against him so there were no grounds for finding him guilty.

Though it wasn't the first time that a black man had been sent to jail unjustly especially not in the New York court system. It *was* the first time that anyone had seen a brothah so skillfully represent his position. So after the shock wore off the courtroom was in an uproar.

The two security guards who sat on each side of the judge's bench immediately ran up to securely move the judge into the judge's chambers. Then two other security guards ran over to grab Nigga. One handcuffed him while the other to the right of him held him tightly by the arm. Then busting through the doors came at least a dozen more security guards who quickly dispersed surrounding the courtroom pews, yanking their guns out of the holsters and aiming them at the crowd to assure that things did not get out of hand.

Black Man

Apparently after Nigga's dynamic closing statement a call was put in for back-up as they anticipated some disruptions.

Nigga remained calm as if not surprised by what had just transpired. Meanwhile, his mother was distraught. With tears streaming down her face she apologized to Nigga with her eyes. Nigga could see the regret in her eyes and so he nodded his head to her in acknowledgement. When he did her legs gave way and she fainted. Shana ran over to help her also looking over at Nigga with apologetic eyes.

Shana knew that she had gone overboard with taking matters as far as getting Nigga criminally charged for non-support. She knew of all the lies and deceitful things that she had done to set the wheels in motion and for that she was sorry. Though as she looked at Nigga sorrowfully Shana knew that sorry was just not good enough. She thought about how she would have to figure out a way to tell her son. Despite all that Shana had done to taint his image of his dad her son still very much loved Nigga. Shana watched Nigga with a regret that she would carry with her for the rest of her life.

What Nigga had said in that courtroom seemed to send a wave of spiritual awareness all across the planet because something strange

Black Man
began to happen soon after. It was something that every melanated person on the planet could simultaneously feel and would eventually experience.

20

All across the planet a wave of Self-awareness swept through all of the melanated people. Simultaneously, they all experienced a sensation of disorientation. They were like bears coming out of hibernation after a dreadfully long, arduous winter.

Throughout the courtroom they all looked around at each other finally recognizing one another for the first time. Even the black security guards felt it and instantly placed their guns back into the holsters. They all began to appear to one another as beams of light.

Moments later currents of energy shot up through their bodies. An invisible force closed then forced their eyes up to their third eye, locked their bodies, sucking the air out of their stomachs causing their chin to rest on their chest followed by a cessation of breath. Then, momentarily they all experienced a shared state of bliss as they all

Black Man

involuntarily began to sing together in an ancient language that would normally have been foreign to them all. As they sang they began to feel the weightlessness of being out of their bodies and then secrets of the universe were revealed to them. They saw the truth about who they were. Next, just as quickly as it had occurred it abruptly came to an end. They all blinked their eyes open and looked around at one another dazed and confused.

    Meanwhile, Nigga stood still unmoved. He didn't seem the least bit surprised by the events that had transpired.   Ironically enough Nigga had dormant memories of having the same experience several times before that in a flash resurfaced. It was an awakening and Nigga had already experienced such a thing several years ago when he first came back into the knowledge of himself.

    During that time Nigga had a vision whereby he saw that he had fallen ill. In the vision he and the others had been stricken with a great illness from which they were unable to ward off. They suffered through one cycle after another trying to heal themselves, but all to no avail. In the meantime, all their struggling to find a cure did was cause the disease to spread more quickly and become more deadly. Before they knew it the disease had gone viral, overtaken them and they had fallen to their death in the land of the dead, the

Black Man

underworld, where the savage race ruled also known as Earth.

So as Nigga looked around at all the faces then staring back at him as if looking for answers, he could only feel shame for having so carelessly brought them with him causing them to also get caught in a prison of his own creation.

Though the underworld had become the savage race's domain it was Nigga's creation so ultimately he would decide what the fate of his world would be. In the knowledge of that Nigga knew that he and the others still had a way out. So he looked out into the crowd with a confident stance and having an expression of knowing that all would be restored.

Seemingly snapping out of their haze the black security guards once again grabbed ahold of their guns aiming them at the crowd in an effort to keep them controlled. Soon after, the two guards that had handcuffed Nigga turned to take him out of the courtroom and out to the prison van to be transported to the station for processing.

As he was ushered out of the back of the courtroom both Shana and Nigga's mother screamed out in agonizing pain. Meanwhile, Nigga's divine queen, his Earth, his Goddess, the only one who truly knew him as she was made of the same cosmic source as he, looked on calmly

Black Man

and without shedding a single tear having shared in Nigga's knowing of what was to come she bid him adieu with a mere nod. Nigga locked eyes with her, sent her one final message and absorbed one last dose of her loving energy before turning around to walk through the door and into the next phase of the battle against the forces within him that were to come and that had initially caused his descent.

Nigga was shoved into the police van and in no time he arrived at the police station where he was processed, booked then taken back into the police van to be transferred to Riker's Island. On the van along with Nigga were other Gods. All knowing the same thing, they each sat quietly communicating through telepathy as to their next course of action. They were all rather anxious to get to Riker's Island as everything was already going exactly according to plan.

At the same time, back at the courthouse the melanated people there were still all abuzz about what had transpired. None of them had any recollection of ever having experienced such a thing. Some of them thought that perhaps they had all been drugged, perhaps through the air vents. Others thought that perhaps they had all imagined it. Then there were others who were totally in denial about any of it and who were acting as if nothing happened. Nonetheless, with what was to

Black Man
come they would all soon remember the truth and then there would be no more questions or doubts.

21

In what seemed like no time Nigga and the others had arrived at Riker's Island. Per the standard procedure, once they arrived the police gave the prison staff Nigga's belongings, he was granted his receipt then strip-searched, forced to shower, given toiletries, clothes and later administered a medical examination. He was then photographed, briefly interviewed, offered one phone call, which he declined, and given an identification badge before being escorted to his cell.

It was late evening by the time Nigga arrived to his cell so it was already lights out, which was exactly the way that he and the others had planned it. They had communicated with one another and agreed that nighttime was the best time for their transformation to take place.

Lots of anticipation was in the air. Nigga had waited so long for that day to arrive as had the others. Meanwhile, the Nagas waited in the wings for their cue. The Nagas had waited patiently for millions of years for the time of their return. Then the day had finally arrived when it was time for the savage race's rule to end and for them to be exterminated. The Nagas had already foreseen that the savage race wouldn't go down quietly though and so they were prepared for a war of great proportions as were Nigga and the others.

Over the years the savage race had become quite strong, which also meant that all the characteristics from which they had been created also grew stronger. So they had become exceptional liars, expert cheats and the most stealthy of thieves.

They had managed to keep the entire race of divine ones in a prison of their own creation without their even knowing it. They even tricked the divine ones into trading places with them.

So the divine ones began to believe that they were the children of the Gods and that the savage race were the Gods. The divine ones began to worship the savage race and hold their savagery ways sacred. The savage race became their lord and master and every aspect of their existence was under the savage race's control.

The savage race had tricked the divine ones into despising everything about themselves and instead loving everything about the savage race.

Black Man

From skin, hair and eye color to cultural differences the divine ones began to hate everything about themselves and instead they developed a strong desire for the attributes of the savage race. In their eyes the savage race had it all. They had desirable looks, money, supreme cultural values, religion and more.

Having successfully tricked the divine ones out of loving themselves the savage race had recruited several agents among the divine ones to carry out their deeds. Agents of the savage race came in all forms. One could never know who one might be. They could have been an office supervisor, celebrity, athlete, preacher, educator or parent. There were agents all around to spread the message of the savage race, which was that the divine ones were inferior. Their message was being aggressively injected into the communities of divine ones all across the planet.

Yet, in order to accomplish a deed of this magnitude most effectively the savage race had to erase every ounce of the divine one's history that it could and they had to be thorough in doing so. If there were any stones left unturned, when the information did surface the savage race would merely lie and create confusion around the information.

Black Man

This resulted in the divine race having a confused perception of who they were and thereby having no knowledge of their own truth. Then whenever they would think that they were finally on the path to discovering their truth they would ultimately realize that it was yet another trick to confuse them. The savage race kept them going around in circles that way for thousands of years.

Like Nigga, the entire race of divine ones were like hamsters on a spinning wheel going nowhere. Collectively the divine ones found themselves trapped and despite how hard they tried to free themselves they remained in the underworld as its prisoners. All that they knew as truth had been stripped away from them and they had been duped into denouncing all remnants of what memories of who they were may have remained.

Then since all melanated persons were not necessarily divine ones those who were had been identified as children then thoroughly examined and closely watched so that the savage race knew exactly how best to contain them at all times. The divine ones were then programmed and told of the new laws that were to be followed before each being given new identities and being escorted away to their new prison life, a prison life from which there was no escape.

Black Man

From there the savage race used a number of tactics to keep the divine ones in a perpetual state of inertia. They gave them movements such as the Civil Rights Movement. They gave them religion. They gave them the battle of the sexes. They gave them systems such as education, culture, government and economies. They gave them germ warfare. Yet the most powerful tactic that they used and that kept the divine ones mentally enslaved was self-hatred. It was self-hatred that would launch an endless cycle of suicide among the divine ones.

Consequently, in the end, all that the savage race had done was put the divine ones in a room of mirrors where they relived the saga of Sutekh, Wasir, Ese, Nebet and Har over and over again. It was a saga in which one person played all the parts. So everything that the main character did while playing the roles of all the other characters ultimately ended up being what he did to himself. It was a dream where all the people in the dream were actually the dreamer. The divine ones were therefore trapped in a dreamworld and the savage race were the gatekeepers.

However, the time had finally come for the dreamers to awaken.....

Black Man

22

In the dead of night at the pinnacle of stillness the transformation began. Then out of the East River they rose again..... the Nagas. All of the melanated Riker's Island prisoners, guards and staff members had involuntarily transformed and awakened as the Nagas.

As a result of their being brainwashed by the savage race many among the divine ones who had also spent some time as the Nagas had forgotten who they were. However, earlier in the day just before Nigga was escorted out of the courtroom when the strange wave of energy swept through everyone, those who were also the Nagas had awakened, including Nigga. It was exactly how the Nagas has planned it. Years earlier when the others left, some of them remained, but in a dormant state unknowingly waiting for their cue to awaken.

This was possible because as several millions of years had passed and the divine ones

Black Man
had cycled through several lifetimes they often reincarnated as different beings, including Nagas. Nigga was one among the divine ones who had done that.

In fact, when he reincarnated back into the underworld as Nigga his self-proclaimed name reflected the part of him that somehow retained some remnants of his memory of being a Naga in a past life. The origin of his name, Nigga, originated from the name Naga. In fact, the name Naga originated from very ancient names which included Niger (one and the same as the country in Africa), which was derived from Negashi, which was derived from Negas, which was derived from Nettyr, which was derived from what was the most ancient derivative, N-G-R (which translated to God as the Nagas were commonly known as the Gods).

Nigga named himself that as he had always felt a strong attraction to the name. It was something that both of his parents hated as they had come up in an era where such a name was perceived as derogatory. However, this was done in ignorance of the true history of the name, which was of course the mind-controlling handiwork of the savage race. So once Nigga began to come into the knowledge of himself, which was shortly after his father left, he renamed himself Nigga. Later, once he became an adult he made the name change legally shocking everyone who had known him. It was a bold move, but as a God it was his nature to such bold things.

As the transformation took place, Nigga couldn't have felt more at home. It felt good to be back in a familiar form in which he felt liberated. The burden of humanity was a weight he preferred not to carry. Nigga had reincarnated as a human more times than he cared to remember, which was probably why he so easily forgot. That was the case with many of the divine ones over the years. Humanity was a burden that, once they remembered, none of them enjoyed the memory of.

Elsewhere in a distant land, from a secret, secured location, an alarm sounded alerting members of the savage race to immediately report to their safety chambers. An emergency broadcast system had been put into place a few hundred years prior to alert their race in anticipation of what all of the savage race knew to be the date of their expiration. Their time was up. They had all been watching the signs and symbols, which told them that it had arrived roughly a thousand years prior.

Nonetheless, they refused to go down without a fight. It was their nature to fight, kill and destroy as they had done and perfected over the course of their entire existence. So they were more prepared than ever for what was to literally be the fight of their life. They did not know the manner in which their extermination would take place. Therefore, they took great care in thoroughly attempting to prepare for anything.

The Nagas were definitely a most worthy opponent. It was known throughout the cosmos that they were in fact, the ultimate predator and their reputation had been well earned. Like the savage race, the Nagas too had their own internal emergency alert broadcast system using a combination of their power of telepathy and mind control. They used those powers to also send out alerts signaling the queens to collect the children and go to safety.

Meanwhile, the Nagas who were spread out all across the planet had slithered out of the waters without having made even the slightest sound. They were all armed and ready to launch the extinction.

There were many whom the divine ones could have called upon for assistance, but their reason for calling on the Nagas was strategically exact. The Nagas had the perfect balance of coldness and righteousness necessary to carry out such a deed. Exterminating one's children would never be easy for the divine ones. However, in the present case it was necessary, which was why the Nagas were called.

As originally predicted by the Nagas the divine ones had finally identified the source of their illness. It was their own jealousy, hatred and disloyalty to one another that caused them to fall.

It initially played itself out in the upper realms at the time of their escape from their enemies when in their shame they began to blame one another. Then it revealed itself again when they further divided, dividing themselves into two genders while living on another planet after having previously existed on a higher frequency that was far beyond gender. After that division, it all became a battle of the sexes where the Gods proclaimed their superiority over the Goddesses losing sight of the necessity for the magnetic attraction of their oppositeness.

Later, on earth while in their lowest form as the black race, after the last stint of their fall the illness presented itself through Wasir's jealousy, hatred and disloyalty toward his brother, which later went viral resulting in Ese's betrayal of her husband and his child, Har. Then the latter display went on to play itself out again and again, lifetime after lifetime, generation after generation all the way into modern times. It seemed that the germ that plagued the divine ones simply refused to die.

Surviving into modern times it displayed itself as the black community's jealousy toward one another in the form of a battle of the sexes and each gender's poor treatment of one another. It also displayed itself as hatred by way of how the black community failed to support one another.

It was well-known throughout the planet that the black community was more than eager to show their undying support for anyone other than their own. This was clearly demonstrated in financial reports which showed that annually the black community spent more than $1.1 trillion on goods and services provided by companies owned and run by races other than their own. Blacks did so despite the fact that they're buying power had been proven to single-handedly fuel the entire world economic system, a system that in no way served them and that continued to carry out its goal of keeping them oppressed.

Next, it displayed itself as disloyalty in how easily many in the black community could be manipulated into turning one another over the enemy and how easily convinced they were to become agents of the enemy. It was the divine one's jealousy, hatred and disloyalty of one another

Black Man

that essentially made them become prisoners of a prison of their own creation.

The Nagas knew it the whole time, but because the divine ones could never see it for themselves despite having already been subjected to so much pain and suffering the Nagas knew that something more devastating would have to happen to force them to see. The Nagas knew that it would take the most catastrophic of experiences to finally open their eyes and so they stepped back and allowed the divine ones to continue down their path of self destruction and it worked.

After the transformation took effect all of the divine ones had finally come into the realization of their illness and simultaneously healed themselves. They did themselves even better by finally coming together, which was the key all the along to their getting back home to the upper realms. Thus, the time had come to rid themselves of their disease once and for all.

23

Quietly the Nigga and the rest of the Nagas moved about the planet in search of their prey. Hunting was a game thoroughly enjoyed by their race and the savage race had proven to be the most difficult to capture, which only heightened the thrill of the hunt. So the Nagas, at the height of their enjoyment, began stalking their prey.

The Nagas had the power to see energy so they were following the energy trails of the savage race. It seemed that in each region they were all gathering into one location. In no time the Nagas had identified all of the secret chambers. Though, since there was no man-made weapon that could stand against the force of the Nagas the so-called security systems that the savage race had in place were of no use. All across the planet the Nagas wiped out entire nations of savages. Though there were still many among the savage race that remained. They were the stronger ones who would not be as easily conquered. Nonetheless, the

Black Man
Nagas were up for the challenge and would still prevail.

Having enjoyed one full night of hunting, which was temporarily enough to quench their thirst and satisfy their palates the Nagas decided to turn in for the day. They each agreed to meet up again the next night to continue on with the hunt. They were nocturnal and the night was their element, but by day they rested.

With lightening speed, Nigga headed home to his queen, Bast. He couldn't wait to be with her. Seeing how she represented for him in court earlier made him want her even more.

Nigga and Bast met each other one day at the get together of a mutual friend's. Jess was Bast's homegirl from college and her boyfriend Shine was Nigga's friend from childhood. It was more like a setup because Jess had been telling Bast about meeting a friend of theirs for some time, but Bast kept declining saying she wasn't into setups.

Nonetheless, once the two eventually met they found themselves together and bonded to one another for life. It seemed the moment they met they were inseparable. They became even more

Black Man

indivisible once they learned how much their lives paralleled, particularly with regards to their spiritual studies.

Bast, like Nigga had been an avid researcher. She was always searching, on a quest to find truth to discover the truth about who she was. Likewise, Nigga always felt that there was something missing in the story that he'd been told about who he was. When he first arrived on Earth he was one who was the most resistant in accepting the lies that the divine ones had been told by the savage race about who they were. Reincarnation after reincarnation, that defiance in Nigga never ceased.

Nigga was different from most, because no matter what all others believed and how much they ostracized him for not following the status quo he would not submit to the manipulation of the savage race. Bast was the same way. No matter what tactics were used neither of their minds could be broken.

It seemed in every way Bast was Nigga's counterpart and so they had an instant connection. He was the one person whom she could confide in as everyone else either could not relate to her, didn't understand why she had to be such a radical freethinker or was secretly plotting against her.

Black Man

When Bast met Nigga she instantly knew that she had realized her God. She believed in him, trusted him, was loyal to him and adored him as her God and him alone. For Bast there was room for only one God in her yoni-verse and Nigga was it.

For Nigga, Bast was the breath of life. Just before he met her he was in the process of battling the court system fighting for the right to be in his children's life. Shana had just started with her antics and JeJaun was pulling her stunts using the children to get back at him for cheating on her.

Nigga having seen something different in Bast from all the rest confided in her about it all. Something within him told him that none of what he had done in his past would run her away and so he bore all, totally exposing himself to her.

She too bore all of her deepest secrets to him exposing all of her flaws, inner demons, weaknesses. hopes, dreams and deepest desires. She didn't care because she felt safe with Nigga. She knew that despite what he had done to the others deep down he was a good man. She knew that she was the divine partner that could bring the God to the surface and that she did.

The closer they became the stronger Nigga grew. He began to remember everything about who he was and within a short time he helped Bast to

Black Man

also remember and soon they both remembered some key aspects of their past lives together.

They both remembered that in a past life Nigga was Sutekh and Bast was Ese and together they ruled as guardian and queen of the heavens. As the memories returned to them they both re-lived the pain that both of them had caused one another. It was an excruciatingly difficult thing to experience again.

However, then being in a better space to address things and forgive one another they were both able to heal one another from the experience. It was a defining moment for them and their union because it was a testament to the strength of their bond.

From there they proceeded to build one another up. They knew that it was the only way that they would find their way out. They figured that even if none of the others could wake up, if they could fully awaken and will themselves to get strong enough to get a message out then they could possibly call for help.

So Bast and Nigga did daily exercises together. They meditated together to become more focused, they used sex magic to enter other realms to communicate with the spirit world and to manifest things that they needed in the physical realm. They also practiced communicating with one another

Black Man

using telepathy as they remembered it once being their primary form of communication.

Bast and Nigga did everything they could think of to awaken at least the slightest inkling of who they were and apparently it worked because they had arrived, answering their call. The Nagas had heard them all the way from the seventh dimension.

It was Nigga and Bast who had contacted the Nagas all those carnations prior to ask for help. They were the couple among the divine ones. Through the power of their love they had done what none of the others could do. Through the power of black love they would finally be able to experience the magnitude of their collective love as they were finally on their way home.

As Nigga had thought about their success, he smiled to himself as he entered their home and slithered up next to Bast before transforming back into his human form.

Black Man

24

Nigga gazed into her eyes whispering to her saying, "Good evening my breathtakingly gorgeous Goddess. How the heaven are you?"

"I'm fine now that my wonder God is here," Bast replied smiling.

Bast wrapped her arms around Nigga and gave him the biggest kiss that the third dimension could contain. Then already knowing what he needed to recharge from all the energy exerted from the hunt when he picked her up she wrapped her legs around him and held him close to her as he carried her into their room where she loved him. She loved him well into the morning then laid him down to enjoy a much needed restful sleep.

Bast knew that everything that had transpired in the courtroom had greatly exhausted Nigga's energy. It took great courage to do what he did in there and as she watched him give his closing statement she knew that all of it had done a number

Black Man

on him. Nigga was one of the strongest of the Gods, but the price of that strength was often an exhaustion of energy. So Bast was sort of like his rechargable battery and it was her pleasure to be that for him.

Like Nigga, as his counterpart, Bast was a very powerful Goddess. While she was most well known as being a great nurturer she was also a fierce protector of the children, which was why Nigga had signaled her immediately after the transformation putting her in charge of making sure the queens collected all of the children and brought them to safety. Bast did not take her responsibility lightly and having absorbed some of Nigga's fiery energy she would often display brute strength in protecting as well as making the others follow out her orders.

Bast complemented Nigga in every way. Where he was hot-tempered she was usually cool and reserved. Where Nigga was the light she was the darkness. While Nigga was all knowing Bast brought him wisdom and together they birthed understanding into the universe. The two of them were quite literally a match made in heaven.

As Bast watched Nigga resting she couldn't help but admire his strength. He fascinated her. He was beauty. He was her heaven. She blushed to herself having been flattered by having been the

Black Man

one lucky enough to be the one to reside at his side. She was the most lucky Goddess in the world.

Nigga slept for several hours. While he slept, Bast went out to all of their safe houses to check on the others and to make sure the children were safe, not that they necessarily needed looking after. As children of the divine ones they had quite the reputation of being more than adequately capable of defending themselves. In fact, they could probably defend the adults better than they could themselves.

The only reason that Nigga and the others did not allow the children to take part in the wars was because at their level of maturity they lacked the self-control necessary to fight in a war. In doing so they would run the risk of losing themselves in the hunt, which would put them at a great disadvantage in the heat of the battle.

So the queens were tasked with ensuring that the children stayed put. Nonetheless, Bast still went around to check on them anyway because some of them were very crafty escape artists.

In fact, Bast arrived at one house to find that there were a couple of children missing. Then soon after she learned that the same thing had happened at at least 5 other houses. Bast knew that the children wanted to take part in the battle and so she

Black Man

knew exactly what had happened. However, many of the queens assured her that they had adequately secured the children and there was no way that any children could have escaped. Instead they informed Bast that they suspected that the children may have been taken by the savage ones.

Bast was infuriated after hearing this news. She knew all too well of the savage race's ways. By then she was sure that the children may have already been killed. She knew that the savage race had probably extracted whatever information they wanted to get out of the children then killed them mercilessly.

Bast immediately headed for home to inform Nigga of the news. She needed to see how he wished to proceed. She knew that she would have to do all within her means to quell his anger over the news so she prepared herself on the way home. Of them both Nigga was quite the fiery one and he would be quite unnerved by this news to say the least. Besides that Bast knew better than anyone of his soft spot for the children.

25

"Peace God," Bast said to Nigga greeting him warmly seeing that he was just waking up when she arrived.

"Good morning sunshine," he said smiling brightly back at her.

"So I was just out checking on things and…. well…" Bast said pausing before continuing.

"What is it? Go ahead and tell me," Nigga replied as if preparing for the worst.

"Some of the children have gone missing," Bast blurted out without hesitating.

"Gone missing?" Nigga questioned as if he was certain that he had not heard her right.

"Yes, God, they've gone missing. I thought that perhaps the children had escaped as you know they are notorious for doing, always trying to make their way into the battles. But I spoke to some of the queens and they said that they don't think that's what happened. They assured me that they had the children very secured and that there was no way they escaped, at least not without help. So they suspect that the children were somehow taken by the savage race," Bast explained.

Then, just as expected Nigga's temper went from 0 to 100 real quick. Bast tried her best to keep him somewhat balanced, which worked to a degree.

"I have to go and gather the others. We have to get those children back before tonight's hunting," Nigga replied with as much calm as he could muster up.

Bast knew that Nigga was only trying to appear calm for her. So she thought it best to let him without calling him out on it, thus irritating him further. She knew that no matter what she said Nigga was going to handle things his way and knowing that he was the guardian of the heavens she knew that in the end he knew best how to go about getting the children back so she left him to what he did best.

She also knew that he wouldn't risk letting his anger get in the way of getting the children back so she didn't worry, but calmly asked him, "What do you need me to do God? How can I help?"

"I need you to go and make sure that the rest of the children are really secure, I mean *really* secure. I know the queens are pretty good at securing them, but I also know what lengths *you* will go to to make sure the children really are secure.

Black Man
You'll go a bit further than the queens. So I would feel a lot better if I knew *you* were the one doing that," Nigga requested.

"I'll do that God. If I have to I'll relocate them all to one of my own safe spots where I *know* the savage race cannot enter. You know where," Bast said signalling Nigga with her eyes.

"Yeah that's a good idea. Go ahead and do that. I gotta go, but I'll meet you back there later," Nigga said before transforming back into his Naga form.

As Bast watched him leave she couldn't help but admire his strength. It was always what attracted her to him since back when they were Sutekh and Ese and nothing had changed. Yet Bast knew that she had her work cut out for her so the moment Nigga left she went to prepare herself.

Once Nigga alerted the others they all fanned out to track down the children's energy scent. They were also still carrying out the extermination. They agreed that if in the process of hunting they came across the scent of any of the missing children they would abandon the hunt and shift their focus to the search. They figured that way the numbers of the savage ones would continue to be reduced making it even easier to track the children.

Black Man

The Nagas were able to sense that the children were still alive, which made them all more optimistic. They could sense that their energy was clustered in one area, which meant that wherever they were they together. The Nagas and the divine ones shared a deep connection so when anything happened to one of them the other felt it.

Nigga having had past lives of being carnated as both Naga and guardian of the heavens was exceptionally skilled in things like locating the missing. He had an uncanny way of thinking like captors. He too had been a captor often being the one to capture some of the most wanted prisoners of war so locating the missing was his specialty.

Nigga channeled those gifts and cleared his mind so that he could more easily focus enough to pinpoint the location of the children without having to do all of the physical roaming to locate them. Unlike all the other Nagas who tracked by physically following the scent, Nigga was able to do so from a fixed location when he was able to focus enough. So he found a quiet spot deep in the forest and focused.

After what seemed like hours Nigga couldn't believe that he hadn't yet located them. The savage ones must have somehow cloaked the place where they were hiding the children. He and all the other Nagas knew that there were a very select few among the savage race who had gone to such great lengths to secure a location. He was sure that they were the ones who had the children and he knew exactly where they were. The savage ones were no doubt keeping the children so that they could be used as a bargaining chip in exchange for their lives when the time came.

Such a tactic was a fantasy that the savage race was allowed the freedom to believe would work, but the fact remained that in the end it would not. Once nightfall hit it was on and the Nagas were more than ready for the hunt and nobody would be spared.

Since the kidnappings had occurred the Nagas took to hunting with ten times more zeal than the night before. By lashing out at them in the manner of kidnapping the divine one's children, the savage had only heightened the thrill of the hunt. Therefore, when they were captured by the Nagas it was way more vicious than anything even the savage race had ever before witnessed.

Then to everyone's surprise within only about two hours after the meeting had commenced, a few of the Nagas had located the children. As soon as they had done so they alerted the others and the rest of the Nagas quickly gathered at the location where the children had been found.

Black Man

    Nigga was especially anxious to learn of the identity of who was responsible for the kidnappings. He also wanted to be sure that the children had not been harmed. He was prepared to issue the kidnapper great pain if the children had in any way been harmed though he doubted it as the children were quite vicious adversaries in their own right. Though when he arrived he was shocked by what he saw.

26

To Nigga and the rest of the Naga's surprise the children had been kidnapped, but it had not been at the hands of the savage race, at least not directly. A few among the divine ones who were still loyal agents of the savage race had kidnapped them.

This betrayal would have to be dealt with and in a very public manner. Disloyalty would not be tolerated under any circumstances. Besides that everyone knew of the finality of Nigga's reckonings with regards to such betrayals. Having been Sutekh in a past life Nigga had issued the most definitive of reckonings to ever go down in the history of the cosmos and he had done so to his own brother for his backstabbing deeds. Since the culprits of this betrayal weren't even of his bloodline there was no telling what the extent of their penance would be.

When Nigga arrived and learned of the identity of the kidnappers he was instantly filled with rage. Having expected him to respond in such a way the others had gathered around him to detain him and in an attempt to suppress his rage. They talked him down and convinced him that they had to deal with the betrayal in the proper way.

Within several minutes Nigga had calmed down enough to at least hear them out then adhere to their requests as he figured it was fair. Meanwhile, the kidnappers were securely detained and taken to the newly secured location of the others. They were put on display for all the others to see to ensure that the message was properly received that such betrayals would not be tolerated.

For the remainder of the night the Nagas continued with the extermination. They hunted with such vigor that they literally exterminated every one among the savage race with the exception of those select few who were still hiding out in an ultra secure location, which the Nagas were still seeking out.

The extermination had almost come to an end and some of the divine ones were already celebrating. Bast was among those celebrating when Nigga arrived.

"Well, well, well if it isn't my champion lover!" Bast said running up to hug him the moment she spotted him in the crowd of Nagas.

Black Man

Still worked up about the traitors who were among them Nigga coldly hugged Bast back. His thoughts were still preoccupied with how the traitors would be discarded.

"Yeah I'm back and the kids too," Nigga said seemingly a thousand miles away.

"Wow don't sound so happy about it God," Bast said sarcastically sensing that Nigga still had some other things on his mind.

"I'm sorry. I am happy that the kids are home. Just have some things heavy on my mind," Nigga replied.

"Ok I see where you are. God I need for you to come back here for a moment. You can at least try to enjoy *this* success. Worry about that other business tomorrow. Some of the queens and I have planned a lavish party for you all for later. Come and go with me so that we can get ready," Bast said grabbing Nigga's hand guiding him toward their room.

Pulling her hand back Nagga said, "Party? This is no time to party. This battle is not yet done. The strongest among them still lives. The party will be on the feast of their corpses and that has not yet been obtained so I suggest that you postpone that party for now," Nigga snapped.

Bast didn't utter another word and simply left Nigga's company to go and inform the others that the party was being postponed. No one questioned it and everyone quickly moved on acting as if there had never even been any mention of a party.

When Bast returned to where the others were gathered outside she wasn't surprised to find that Nigga had left. She headed to their room as she already knew that it was exactly where she would find him brewing over the night's events.

During times like those Nigga liked to be away from the others. Since they were in lots of company in their hidden location Bast knew that Nigga would be searching for a place that was quiet, where he could enjoy some solace.

Finding Nigga in their room looking out the window Bast walked through the door saying half playfully in an attempt to lighten his mood, "Hmmm how did I *know* that I'd find you here?"

"You *do* know me best. Sorry for snapping at you back there. It's been a really long day and I guess I'm still a bit worked up. I'm really just as ready as you are to celebrate, but we've been stuck in this prison so long that before I start celebrating and breaking out the forties and half pints I just need to make sure that we have rid ourselves of this germ once and for all," Nigga explained.

"You know you don't need to explain that to me. I totally understand. I feel the same way. I guess I just got caught up in the moment. We've

Black Man

never been this close to getting out of here before. It's been so long since we tasted true freedom that we're all just feeling a bit of a blood-lust thirst for it if a hunter like yourself can understand what I mean," Bast responded smiling up at Nigga.

"Oh I share the same blood-lust my love. In fact, I'm feeling a rush of it coming on right now," Nigga said creeping up behind Bast playfully grabbing her by the lower waist.

"Ha ha ha! I just bet your are. Well I suppose it would be okay for us to go ahead and enjoy a private mini celebration of our own for now," Bast said as Nigga moved in to kiss her on the neck.

"I wholeheartedly agree. Let the party begin," Nigga said as he gently laid Bast down on their bed.

The two of them must have "celebrated" for hours. The sun was setting by the time they finally threw in the towel and decided to get some sleep. Then when it seemed they had only been asleep for mere minutes there was a sharp, urgent knock at the door.

27

Looking over at one another, without saying anything Nigga and Bast jumped up and got dressed. They already knew what the knock at the door was about. The savage ones had struck back.

Nigga went on and answered the door and it was one of the Nagas coming to tell him that just as they had planned the traitors had gotten away and the savage ones had just launched their first oounter-attack. Nigga was not concerned as he was happy to see that everything was going according to plan.

Only those in the inner circle knew of the Nagas true hunting strategies. The Nagas had actually staged the escape. They did it to draw out the identity of any possible traitors. If any were identified the penalty would most certainly be swift death.

Traitors could always easily be identified because they were so predictable. If anyone came

Black Man

forward to try to help the staged traitors escape then the Nagas would know that there was still some trace of the illness amidst the divine ones and action would have to be taken to more thoroughly cure them of it.

However, there were no attempts to rescue the "traitors" which assured the Nagas that the divine ones were finally cured. As protectors of the higher realms it was the responsibility of the Nagas to make sure that beings were not infected with any form of disease before being granted passage.

They were very thorough in their examinations as they took their jobs very seriously. Thus far, the divine ones were clear for passage and all that remained to be done was the final extermination of the last of the savage ones. Then a harmonious existence would once again be restored and any who came to live on Earth any time in the future would be able to do so peacefully.

Letting Bast know that he was leaving for the final hunt, Nigga transformed into his Naga form and went to join the others so that he could finally take care of the savage race once and for all. Meanwhile, Bast and the other queens began to get everyone ready for departure. Everyone was beaming with excitement, all except Bast. Like Nigga she just could not allow herself to be excited until the last of them was gone. Thoughts of the hellish reality that they had all endured began to flood her mind.

Bast saw flashes in her mind of all the genocides that had occurred, the horrors of 200 plus years of slavery in the Americas, the hideousness of Apartheid, the massacres of their leaders, the sadistic, inhumane crimes committed against the divine ones, the killing of innocent black children, campaigns launched to murder their minds and kill their spirits and the ruthless attempts to erase all physical evidence of their history. Earth was by far the most hellish reality in existence and yet they had survived it. Bast looked around admiring the bravery and strength of those around her who were among the survivors. She was in awe of them. They had endured lifetime after lifetime of being hated by everyone else in the world, tortured, beaten and raped of their divinity.

Then in the midst of her thoughts it started again. The others looked at one another as they began to feel it surge through them as well. Moments later their eyes involuntarily snapped shut and their eyes made way to their third eye. The air was sucked out of their stomach, their chins fell to their chest and then breathing all about them ceased. They all locked minds and joined as one mind with the Nagas, together they located the last

Black Man

of the savage race. It was divinely right that they all took them out together, as one.

As the divine ones all looked around at the few remaining members of the savage race they recognized them as having been their primary oppressors. Lifetime after lifetime they had each returned with the sole purpose of inflicting blow after blow and jab after jab upon each and everyone of the divine ones who presently had the last of their fates in the palm of their hand.

It was a mirror that was difficult to look into, but that was the only means of their cure. As the divine ones watched the savage race survivors with their sorrowful, apologetic faces none among the divine ones agreed that they deserved such an easy way out as simple as death. Death was too gracious a penalty. The Nagas agreed as did many among the other Gods and Goddesses.

However, the savage race was a disease that had to be eradicated and having finally arrived at the point where such a thing was even an option seemed to be the universe's gift to them. Who were they to look a gift horse in the mouth?

With that the divine ones, while locking minds with the Nagas, soaked in the thrill of the hunt as they struck within an instant each wrapping themselves around those who remained of the savage race. As the Nagas wrapped around them,

Black Man

hearing the crushing of their bones the divine ones also symbolically heard the crushing of what remained of the their horrific memories of life on Earth.

Then as their prey took in it's last breath so did the divine ones. It would be that last breath that the divine ones ever again breathed into their life among the dead. The dead bodies of the savage ones went limp and simultaneously the divine one rose up, levitating, each coming to life and once again back into consciousness leaving the Nagas to feast on the corpses of who had been their most sought after prey.

28

When it was all done Nigga anxiously returned to Bast smiling ear to ear with a smile that was brighter than sunshine. The moment she saw him she ran up to him and gave him a hug that was bigger than the universe.

"So are you ready to party now my love?" Bast asked smiling.

"Do you have to ask? And I hope ya'll got all the trimmings for a real party, black folks style, cause this party needs to last for a least a few million years! So break out the bubbly, the forties, the pints, the joints, the grill, the cards, the dominoes, the horseshoes and the shit-talking. Then prepare *our* room with all of my favorite outfits with the blessing that is your ass out because I don't know how long *we're* gonna be *partying*!" Nigga said excitedly.

"Wow you're funny! You are really funny! And you know what? I already did all of that! Stop acting like you know me God," Bast said smiling.

Black Man

"Oh I'm not acting. You know who I am. Now get over here and *show* me that you know who I am!" Nigga ordered.

Then just like Nigga said they all partied for what seemed like millions of years until the cycle came around again for their fall. Then when they needed them, the Nagas came to the rescue again with Nigga leading the way.

The Nagas were the serpent warriors Gods who invoked the cycle of death and rebirth. They brought with them the spirit of renewal and resurrection. They were the most fearless defenders and protectors of the higher realms and even today they are still among us.

You can recognize them by their fearless disposition, the power of their minds, their ability to endure in the face of adversity, their courageousness and most certainly by their secret symbol. They are the unbound. You know them because not even the curse of this world can bind them. They are those that live by the code of truth, justice and righteousness. They are the ones that can only be seen with the 3rd eye. They can only be perceived through the subconsciousness and they can only be conceptualized from the upper realms.

They are the Gods who became the damned only to rise again. They bear the name that many

Black Man
are afraid to speak aloud. Shhhhhhhhhh…... They are…

The "N" word. **N-G-R** (God). **Net-tyr**. **Negus**. **Negashi**. **Niger**. Negre. Negro. Nigger. "What up my nigga!" "Nigga please!" "No Niggers allowed." "Be a good nigger and do as you're told." "Niggas ain't shit!" "That's that nigga shit." "Nigga you betta back up off me!" "Fuck that nigga!" "I ain't yo nigga bitch!" "Look at that stupid nigger." "Who the fuck you think you callin a nigga!" "Dat's my nigga!" "That bitch ass nigga!" "Sup nigga?" "What's cracka lackin nigga?" "Wuzup niggas?" "You's my nigga!" "My nigga, long time no see." "Faggat ass nigga," "Nigga stop fakin."

They are rising now from the primeval waters of YOU…. Niggas of the world rise! Rise Niggas! Rise!!!

Black Man

(To Be Continued)

If you enjoyed this book or received value from it in any way, then I'd like to ask you for a favor. Would you be kind enough to leave a review for this book on Amazon? It'd be greatly appreciated!

About the Author....

Amirah Bellamy is truly a bonafide artist of many crafts. In addition to being a novelist she's also a Kemetic yoga instructor and singer (check out her cd entitled "Raising Love Consciousness also available on Amazon). Amirah grew up in the DC Metro area, which is where much of the inspiration to many of her novels came from. She developed a fondness for the sci-fi genre as a child watching shows like Star Trek and movies like Star Wars. Eventually, her fascination with the metaphysical evolved into research, which then evolved into novel writing. Today, as a novelist she now welcomes you into her creative universe.

To learn more about Amirah Bellamy

email.... amirahbellamy@gmail.com
or
visit..... www.EthericRealmsInv.com

Black Man

Other books by this author also available (Visit www.EthericRealmsInv.com to learn more!) ....

Black Man

Black Man

www.ingramcontent.com/pod-product-compliance
Lightning Source LLC
Chambersburg PA
CBHW071429180526
45170CB00001B/267